AN ENGLISH ALMANAC

*An introduction
to the English Year,
its calendar, traditions,
anniversaries,
and events*

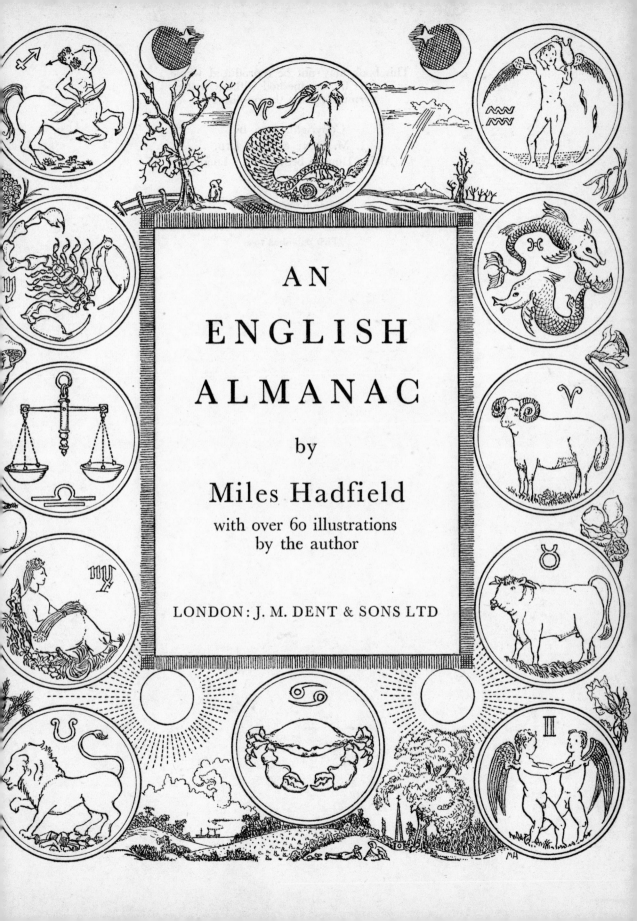

AN
ENGLISH
ALMANAC

by

Miles Hadfield

with over 60 illustrations
by the author

LONDON: J. M. DENT & SONS LTD

Copyright, 1950, by
J. M. DENT & SONS LTD.
Aldine House · Bedford St. · London

Made in Great Britain
by
The Temple Press · Letchworth · Herts
First published 1950

PREFACE

I SUPPOSE a calendar is much the same the world over—a 'plot' on paper of the anticipated occurrence, or mostly recurrence, of events in natural time, for the 'purpose' (as the dictionary has it) of civil life! It is like a skeleton or scaffolding projecting into the future which, as time passes, will be covered by the living flesh of happenings or become draped and decorated with memories.

An almanac is this skeletal calendar, not clothed with life itself, but with some representation or description of the events which form the flesh and its drapery. This covering can, of course, be devised and arranged according to the whim of the compiler, and it therefore comes about that an almanac is not only a calendar dressed up, but one dressed to go somewhere.

Thus, we are told, the first almanacs consisted of clogs or blocks of wood, the corners being notched with the days according to the calendar. On the flat sides the first compiler did his almanackery when he drew symbols of the Christian festivals and related them to the notches which gave their dates. Many and various—and indeed famous—are the successors to this simple idea. Most are practical and useful aids to our complicated existence, but they have been invented to serve numerous purposes. The first to be printed was, it is said, produced by Regiomontanus in 1472. Subsequently they have streamed from the press, ranging from the laudable old *British Almanac*, issued by the Society for the Diffusion of Useful Knowledge, to that multitude of publications, equally full of useless knowledge and superstition, with such titles as *Prognostication Everlasting of Right Good Effect*, *Merlinus Anglicus Junior*, *Bloody Almanac*, *Merlinus Redivivus*, and *Poor Robin*, all of which had their seasons of success and popularity between the sixteenth and nineteenth centuries.

Then there have been numerous specialized almanacs—nautical, poetical, astronomical, and the famous *Almanach de Gotha*, which told of the ancient families and states of Europe.

This little book is an almanac particularly directed to displaying those features of the passage of time peculiar to the English and England, with its fresh, moist countryside and grimy towns.

v

If he listened only to our conversations in buses and trains, or read only the headlines in our newspapers, the stranger might draw quite false conclusions about our own private almanackery.

First, he would assume that our principal concern was with the manifestations of our climate. He would learn that we were usually suffering the worst weather on record, or, in fine weather, the finest spell ever, or, more probably, one that we 'shall make up for later on.'

Next in importance he would find Sport. Printed in heavy type in the calendar he would expect to find the dates of the opening of the seasons for soccer and the various brands of horse-racing. Great events (it would seem to an outsider) are few: *The* Cup, *The* Boat Race, *The* National, and *The* Derby. The plutocracy also like their fellow citizens to be aware when certain game, fish, pests, or vermin can be destroyed in a manner becoming to a gentleman.

Then our festivals. There are apparently only two: *A* Happy Christmas, and *The* Bank Holiday.

Or our history and anniversaries of great men and events. Only one stands out—the unsuccessful attempt made by Guy Fawkes to blow the foundations of democracy up into the sky. A smaller number of people will recall Trafalgar Day or The Death of Nelson.

The Englishman, too, has a reputation as a lover of nature, though from our newspapers the stranger would believe that we only take account of hearing the first cuckoo in spring.

Possibly the visitor to our island may think that the works of our poets (which, we are now assured, remain the only part of our achievement which is internationally considered to be a moderate success) have become current in our talk. But he would be wrong, for probably the only line he will hear quoted in Shakespeare's country will be 'Oh, to be in England now that April's there' as a cold rain from the north blots out the green haze of the breaking buds.

But, as has so effectively been shown in the past, we are a misleading race, partly because we forget to tell other people much about our affairs; indeed, we are liable to forget about them ourselves. A little further inquiry will soon show that there really is rather more clothing to the framework of our calendar than those few simple rags of newspaper and daily gossip.

I have, therefore, collected and arranged some of these additional items under the same headings, but in a slightly more decorous order than the examples that I have quoted above.

After a polite introduction to the month we must, like the party in the Holyhead mail, first approach the various knotty points of meteorology, which usually form the exordium of an English conversation. These being discussed and exhausted and the ice being thus broken, the colloquy may—as it did with travellers—ramble to other topics.

The first of these will be our feasts and festivals, which must just take precedence over our sports, which in turn just gains priority of discussion over the more elementary facts of our natural history.

Next come our anniversaries of events, epochs, and records. The last two now appear to be of more importance than in days gone by. Formerly epochs were only made occasionally, such as by the Normans or the discovery of electricity. Modern society is, however, rather an improvement, and with the help of the daily press we manage to make an epoch most days. The same with records; we ask of practically every happening, 'Is this a record?' and, of course, from some considerations it nearly always is, which is immensely satisfactory. I have, therefore, included notes on the making of some epochs and also a monthly record or two.

Finally some observations on the calendar made by our poets are included.

Each month is decorated with symbols that are, I hope, appropriate. In addition, I have searched among my sketch-books and devised pictures representative of each—in the country, the city, or, where most of us live to-day, the suburb.

An almanac is the one kind of book in which originality of thought or imagination must be avoided—unless it be one of those guides to the more problematical likelihoods of the future, which this is not. That means that all the information I give has been taken, lock, stock, and barrel, from some standard authority, some dull statistical work, or from old newspapers or magazines. These sources have taught me much and entertained me greatly and I am heavily in their debt.

It would be ungrateful if I did not acknowledge it to William Hone and Robert Chambers among the ancients, and the delightful writings of Miss Christina Hole and Mr. Laurence Whistler among the moderns.

I should add here that whenever two versions of a story or an incident exist I have invariably chosen the more picturesque. Sport and Natural History have, of course, been treated with due solemnity and accuracy.

Perhaps, too, I should warn the reader that I do not write as an expert, still less as a scholar, but only as a somewhat opinionated and certainly haphazard 'browser.'

I must mention certain omissions. As is not unusual developments have taken place quite recently which, by their supporters, are said to inaugurate unprecedented eras and magnificent epochs. Others disagree quite strongly with this view. In view of the doubt—and in any case I should hate to confuse an era with an epoch—these happenings have been left out.

M. H.

CONTENTS

ACKNOWLEDGMENTS

THANKS are due to the following authors and publishers for permission to reprint copyright material:

The Society of Authors and Mrs. Binyon for 'August Weeds' from *The Collected Poems of Laurence Binyon*; Miss Margaret T. Carleton for W. S. Blunt's 'St. Valentine's Day'; the Clarendon Press for 'January' and 'North Wind in October' from *The Poetical Works of Robert Bridges*; Mr. Richard Church for 'Robin' from *The Glance Backward*; Mr. Walter de la Mare and Messrs. Faber & Faber Ltd. for 'Winter' from *Poems 1901–1918*; Mrs. W. H. Davies and Messrs. Jonathan Cape Ltd. for 'April's Charm' from *The Collected Poems of W. H. Davies*; the Oxford University Press for 'July' from *The Complete Poetical Works of Austin Dobson*; Messrs. Sidgwick & Jackson Ltd. for 'Summer's End' from *The Collected Poems of John Drinkwater*, iii; Mr. Vivian L. Ellis for 'The Cuckoo'; Miss Eleanor Farjeon for 'March Blow By'; Mrs. Freeman and Messrs. Macmillan & Co. Ltd. for John Freeman's 'November Skies'; Messrs. Macmillan & Co. Ltd. and the Trustees of the Thomas Hardy Estate for 'An August Midnight' from *The Collected Poems of Thomas Hardy*; the representative of W. E. Henley and Messrs. Macmillan & Co. Ltd. for 'Ballade of June'; Mr. Milton Waldman for Robert Nichols's 'November' from *Aurelia*; the Clarendon Press for Sir Arthur Quiller-Couch's 'Upon New Year's Eve'; Messrs. Michael Joseph Ltd. for Miss V. Sackville-West's 'March' from *The Garden*; Sir Francis Meynell and Messrs. Burns, Oates & Washbourne Ltd. for Francis Thompson's 'July Fugitive.'

AN ENGLISH ALMANAC

JANUARY  CAPRICORNUS

JANUARY, the first month, has thirty-one days. Besides being the brand-new, shiny month in a still untarnished year, it is comparatively a newcomer to the calendar. The mythical Romulus, who founded Rome and invented the original system of dividing years into months, made only ten of them. These included 304 days. What happened to the remaining $61\frac{1}{4}$ is a mystery. Numa Pompilius, a philosopher who was elected to follow Romulus as king, saw that something was wrong, and added two more. One, January, was put at the beginning of the year.

The month is named after Janus, who some said, was a king of Latium. Deification caused him to develop two faces. As deity of the month one looks back to the old year, the other forward.

It is also in some ways an innovation as the first month in our own calendar. Until 1752, for legal and other purposes, the year began on 25th March.

The Anglo-Saxon name for January was Wulfmonath, the month when the wolves starved and descended ferociously on villages. Wolves were exterminated in our islands by the middle of the eighteenth century, but progress has not been able to change the weather. Cold and dark, often frosty and with more slush than snow, it often seems much longer than its days.

But let us picture the month optimistically through the eyes of people vigorous in mind and body. It is white with snow, which sparkles dimly as it catches the light from the low sun. A sheet of black, glassy ice has been swept clear for the skaters. Around the pool are patterns of bare trees and sheltering rhododendrons, their leaves curled by the crisp frost.

THE WEATHER

The greatest cold of winter generally follows the winter solstice by some three weeks. January is, therefore, usually the coldest month in the year. But it is not usually very wet, the average rainfall making it about the sixth wettest month of the year.

The coldest day of the year by tradition falls on the feast of St. Hilary. This is kept by the English Church on the 13th and the Roman on the 14th. It was on the 14th January that the historic frost of 1205 began, which lasted until 22nd March. But that was with the old-style calendar. Until the middle of the eighteenth century it was not very remarkable for the Thames to be frozen over. Evelyn tells of this happening in his January diary both for 1649—when there were also 'horrid tempests of wind'—and for 1695.

The most bitter day recorded in and around London was on 20th January 1838, when the thermometer fell to $-14°$ F., or $46°$ of frost.

On the other hand, Pepys tells us how in one January there was 'a fast day to pray for more seasonable weather, it having been like May or June.' In 1825 we read that so mild was it that a blackbird's nest had been found with eggs in it; a more substantial record is $64°$ F. reached in London on 23rd January 1828—a figure that has not been exceeded. In the cold spell of 1940 rain fell on the evening of the 27th and froze almost at once. The result was an 'ice-storm,' which felled and mutilated thousands of trees.

The normal temperature is about $39°$ F.

The weather on St. Paul's Day, 25th January, has long been famous for its qualities of prognostication:

> If St. Paul's be fair and clear,
> It doth betide a happy year;
> But if it chance to snow or rain,
> Then will be dear all kinds of grain;
> If clouds or mists do dark the sky,
> Great store of birds and beasts shall die;
> And if the winds do fly aloft,
> Then wars shall vex the kingdom oft.

THE HEAVENS

On or about the 1st is the latest time of sunrise during the year. At the beginning of the month the sun is in the sign Capricornus, the goat, but passes into Aquarius, or the Water-carrier, on or about the 21st.

FEASTS, FAIRS AND FESTIVALS

1st January. New Year's Day. The Circumcision.

This has lost all its former glory. Once it was a great day for present giving, particularly from loyal subjects to their sovereign. This seems to have been particularly so in Elizabethan and Jacobean times. The giving of gloves, or glove money, was specially associated with the occasion.

At Queen's College, Oxford, the bursar hands each fellow a needle threaded with silk with the words 'Take this and be thrifty.' The ceremony is said to be connected with the name of the founder of the college, de Eglesfield, and a play on words in the phrase *aiguille et fil*.

In some places God-cakes were made and sold for the day. At Coventry they were triangular and filled with mincemeat.

The Feast of the Circumcision was first celebrated by the Church in the eighth century. It gave respectability to earlier pagan customs.

New Year's Day in the old-style calendar fell upon what is now the 13th.

2nd January.

At Ringwood in Hampshire free loaves were given to all the poor who cared to fetch them.

6th January. The Epiphany of our Lord or Twelfth Night.

This day ends the great feast of Christmas; in ancient days the northerners could now see the first sign of lengthening days, and knew that by degrees light and life were returning to earth, and a new cycle of growth to harvest had really begun.

6

So the old Church, very early in its history, attached to it the Feast of the Epiphany, or the manifestation to the men from the east that the infant Christ was far more than a future King of the Jews.

As the last of the twelve days of Christmas it is the day when all decorations must be taken down.　The maidens of the house would see a goblin for every leaf left hanging.

The feast is now almost forgotten except by the devout.　Once it was one of those days for wassailing apple-trees, particularly in the south-west.　In Herefordshire the wassail bowl was taken to the cow-byre and the red-and-white Hereford cattle were toasted.

During the last century London children treated it rather like the 1st of April and played practical jokes.　At that time the 'epiphany' was a display in the pastry-cooks' shops, particularly of masterpieces in icing sugar.　The innocent gazer was liable to find when he moved away that his coat-tails had been pinned to the window frame.　The Twelfth Day cake has now disappeared; but other epiphanies remain for those simple enough to see them.

This was Christmas Day in the old calendar, when the thorn-tree at Glastonbury used to flower.　Unlike many other miraculous happenings it refused to change its habits when the calendar was altered.　The thorn sprang from the staff carried by Joseph of Arimathea when he visited this country.　Its offspring still grow and flower at Orcop in Herefordshire and elsewhere.

At Haxey in Lincolnshire there exists a ritual game, perhaps better called a scramble, for an object called the Haxey Hood.　The winner who eventually gains it enters one of three old public houses, which finishes the game, and all that remains is general celebration of victory.　The 'hood' represents a cloak supposed to have been dropped by a certain Lady Mowbray in the thirteenth century.　Probably its origin is much older; it may be a survival of the scramble for pieces of the sacrificial meat which were thrown to the crowd.

A more recent custom is the Twelfth-Night ceremony at Drury Lane theatre. The attendants, wearing their eighteenth-century livery and wigs, carry a cake into the green-room.　There it is formally cut and distributed to the company of players acting at the theatre.　The custom comes from a bequest made by Baddeley on his death in 1794.　He was a chef who became actor.

The tale goes that once he cooked a very fine dinner for the actor Foote, who asked him what he would like as a reward. Baddeley asked for and got a part in the next play and so started his career on the stage.

Until 1758 the king, attended by the Heralds and Knights of the Orders of the Garter, the Thistle, and the Bath, offered gold, frankincense, and myrrh at the altar of the Royal Chapel in St. James's Palace. After that date and to this day the offering is made on the king's behalf by two gentlemen ushers attended by Yeomen of the Guard.

In the old-style calendar Epiphany fell on what is now the 17th.

7th January. St. Distaff's Day.

The saint is the distaff of the women who return to their spinning after the twelve days. In the evening the men on returning from the fields tried to seize and burn all the flax and tow belonging to their women-folk. The women retaliated by dowsing the flames and men with pails of water, and a rude rustic contest developed between the ancient elements of fire and water.

8th January. St. Lucian.

He was an ascetic who devoted his life to the study of scripture. Supporting himself as a writer he lived at Antioch, where he became a presbyter. Eventually, during a wave of persecution, he was tortured and died bravely persisting in his faith in 327.

Though quite an important saint little tradition seems to have been gathered around him. He was born at Samosata, whence also came the great heathen essayist of the same name.

13th January. St. Hilary.

This day recalls Hilarius Pictarius, Bishop of Poitiers; it is the anniversary of his death about 368. Though the English Church keep it as a festival the Roman Church for administrative reasons chose the 14th. Thus there is some confusion.

Hilary was apparently a young man of fashion who embraced Christianity. He became famous as a debater on the disputed points of the early Christian sects. Rather unusually for a saint, he died a natural death calmly.

There is a tradition that his day is the coldest in the year.

14th January.　Hunting the Mallard.

This custom is observed once a century at All Souls College, Oxford. It is said that when workmen were digging the college foundations in 1438 they disturbed a mallard, which they chased. A symbolic hunt now takes place, led by a Lord Mallard, who is elected from among the fellows. It falls due next in 2001.

17th January.　St. Anthony.

St. Anthony was a young man of Egypt who inherited a very large fortune which he felt it right to distribute to the poor. He himself lived an ascetic life, for a time in solitude, when his celebrated temptations by the devil were resisted. Disciples flocked to his retreat in the Fayum and built their cells in his neighbourhood. This formed the first monastic community and he thus became adopted as the patron saint of monks. He died in 356 over a hundred years old.

His name is also connected with the cure of skin diseases, particularly 'St. Anthony's fire,' or erysipelas.

Wassailing of apple-trees prevailed on this day long after the calendar had changed the date of Epiphany.

19th January.　St. Wulfstan.

This charming old gentleman—he died at a great age, the last of the saints of the Anglo-Saxon Church, in 1095—was Bishop of Worcester and closely concerned with the origin of that cathedral. He was kind and homely; once he became so greatly engrossed in cooking a goose for his dinner that he forgot to keep an appointment to preach a sermon. He forswore meat ever after.

His day is still celebrated at Worcester.

20th January.　The Eve of St. Agnes.

By fasting, maidens could induce dreams of their future husbands. The custom is described by Keats:

> . . . upon St. Agnes' Eve,
> Young virgins might have visions of delight,
> And soft adorings from their loves receive
> Upon the honey'd middle of the night,
> If ceremonies due they did aright;

As, supperless to bed they must retire,
And couch supine their beauties, lily-white;
Nor look behind, nor sideways, but require
Of heaven with upward eyes for all that they desire.

21st January. St. Agnes.

A virtuous Roman maiden who was cruelly persecuted and finally suffered martyrdom under the rule of Diocletian; she is said to have been only twelve or thirteen years old at the time. A basilica still stands on the spot where she died.

St. Agnes has long been the patroness of purity. Perhaps because of a play on names, her festival was associated with sheep. One was decorated and led in the procession taking place at her commemoration. Later it was the practice to bless the sheep on this day.

25th January. The Conversion of St. Paul.

The miraculous conversion of St. Paul has long been honoured by the Churches. During the thirteenth century it was a holiday. There is little popular superstition connected with it other than its significance to weather prophets.

THE SPORTSMAN

The sports proper to the month are undoubtedly skating and, in the north, curling.

Over most of our islands skating out of doors is a chancy affair; how many times do we learn that the racing events in the Fens are abandoned because of a thaw within a few hours of the announcement that they are about to be held? But thanks to our ice-palaces and the comparative proximity of Switzerland, skating is now a popular sport in spite of our climate.

But it is skating of a very different kind from that known to our forefathers. On black ponds they sailed erectly and rigidly around an orange, patiently cutting their neat figures in a dignified manner—the comparison with great black rooks calmly wheeling has been made. Then in 1898 Britain was allotted the third world's championship in the new international style.

Dash, speed, science, and skill soon won the day; dazzling and graceful spectacle replaced formal dignity.

Curling has been described as bowls on ice, a 40-lb. block of granite replacing the 'wood.' It is an ancient game, Holland and Scotland both claiming its origin. Official rules were first drawn up at Edinburgh in 1838.

Greatest excitement is no doubt provided by the early rounds of the Football Association Challenge Cup. The big clubs have begun battling in earnest.

The crews of the boats for the Oxford and Cambridge race are now photographed training on their local waters.

A number of steeplechase meetings are held, including the well-known Hurst Park meeting in the middle of the month.

THE NATURALIST

There are but few Januarys that do not give us a week or so of fair weather when we can feel and not only see that life is seizing every chance to return to earth. Such intimations come when the low sun shines on the edge of a wood, a pale blue sky overhead, rather low clouds being blown over it by a south-west wind. There is the persistent, strident, metallic ring of the great-tit as it goes so ostentatiously and energetically about its business. The first hazel-nut catkins have ceased to be rigid, tight-packed cylinders, and become loose danglers full of dusty pollen, which falls on to the little crimson feelers that protrude from the embryo nut—so like some marine animal that one expects them to be withdrawn at a touch. The hazel flowers over a long period, and the opening of the catkins has been much studied by botanists and meteorologists (who use the event in their time-tables). Bushes start pollinating at different times, some much earlier than others, and oddly enough this is not entirely connected with the situation, for one in a warm, sheltered spot is quite likely to be a late flowerer.

In the open places on the floor of the wood several signs of spring can be found. Celandine, wood anemone, and ground elder leaves will be appearing, and possibly the snouts of bluebells. Sycamore seedlings, with their two or sometimes three cotyledons expanded, are sure to have made a start if the weather is mild; in the mould many acorns will have started their long tap-roots driving deep into the ground.

Honeysuckle bines are sure now to bear tender-looking green leaves, and the bronze buds of elder seem, as almost always in late winter, just ready to break.

Given a mild season the garden may have much more to show; even in a cold year forking the borders shows how close to the surface are blue-bells, crocus, and daffodil leaves. Some of the early crocuses may be had in flower—*Imperati,* with big flowers of buff and purple, and the little *Chrysanthus,* in all shades between gold and white. Hardy though they are, wind and rain make them look rather sad. The dwarf daffodil *Asturiensis* from the Pyrenees is tougher, and nearly always provides a few yellow, toy daffodils before the month is over. But most rewarding is the Algerian iris, *Unguicularis* (the ugly name refers to the claw-like petals), which will throw up many flowers if it is placed in some dry, sunny, poverty-stricken bit of ground—best of all at the

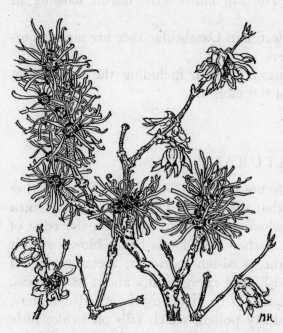

Chinese Witch-hazel and Winter-sweet

base of the wall. The long, brittle-stalked buds if pulled from right down at their bases will open into rather fugitive lilac flowers in water; easy though the plant is, few people grow it. But most surprising of all is the witch-hazel brought from China in Victorian times. There are many people still left to gasp on seeing it for the first time—a tall, open shrub covered, even in icy weather, with thousands of bright yellow flowers, each made up of a tuft of little ribbons held in a crimson cup. Not quite so gay, but immensely fragrant, is winter-sweet, another Chinaman introduced nearly two hundred years ago, but rarely seen. The waxy flowers, glistening and translucent, are beautiful when seen close to. Some bush honeysuckles also scent the air, but their insignificant flowers are quite unlike our own woodbine. White Christmas roses are usually out, and winter heliotrope (*Petasites fragrans*) is another scent-giver with dingy flowers. It is more or less naturalized in some places. But we must quit winter gardening, leaving many other plants undescribed. While to the adventurous and ingenious gardener it is often (but not always) a rewarding pastime, it is to the glass-house gardener that most of us look—to-day we have hyacinths, tulips, daffodils, anemones, cyclamen, azaleas, and many other gay flowers mass-produced for our benefit to cheer the darkest January day.

For the bird-watcher this is a month when birds combine into flocks. He does better if the weather is cold and stormy. At home, if it is, then the bird-table is a powerful attraction, and rare visitors can be watched. For the traveller, river estuaries that remain unfrozen become the feeding-ground of vast crowds of birds. Even streams and ponds in the comparative shelter of gardens will, in extreme weather, draw unusual visitors, such as herons and snipe. If the arctic storms are bad we read of rare visitors—fabulous white-tailed sea-eagles and snowy owls.

Apart from the robin and great-tit the missel-thrush is the most cheerful singer. But on fair, sunny days the song-thrush may give us one of the real sounds of spring.

On the farm lambs are born, and we may hear a lark over the fields. Otherwise winter work continues. The ubiquitous tractor has now taken over the threshing-machine, and we have lost the peaceful hum that used so often to drift over the January air in the days of steam.

Of our animals some of the slumberers may be seen—squirrels, badgers, or the hedgehog, who takes a last run round before settling down finally at the end of the month to sleep without break until the warm April sun rouses him.

Flies, happily, have now almost entirely disappeared, though gnat-like creatures will always be found dancing in a column if the weather calls them out. Hibernating butterflies are very seldom seen, but the dull winter moth is about, and joined by *Theria rupicapraria*, whose proper season it is, and whose arrival is noted as a seasonal landmark by those who study such things. The male is a dull enough creature, the female duller still—a crawler without wings. Those caterpillars living in the ground are, of course, quite often

13

active, and 'cutworms' come up at night—particularly in cold frames—and devour any foliage that there is.

Brown Owl

Many unseasonable sights are to be seen in some years when the early winter has been mild, and letters are sent to newspapers about them; these are 'left-overs' and do not belong to the new year. One letter to the editor of *The Times* of 12th January 1950, describing how a humming-bird hawk-moth was seen flying round the lights at Charing Cross station, is, however, worth recording as an instance of what January can provide. But nearly all such signs are fallible portents of spring. The very depth of winter lies in the heart of the month; darkness, snow, and ice may still cover the earth for most of its days, and only the owl is abroad.

ANNIVERSARIES, EPOCHS, AND RECORDS

7th January 1785. The first aerial crossing of the Channel was made in a balloon. M. Blanchard accompanied by his American backer, Dr. Jeffries, rose from a field near Dover Castle; they only just made the French coast, jettisoning even the wine in their endeavours to remain airborne.

7th January 1804. *The Times* leader page was first headed with the figure of a clock showing 6.6 a.m.—the normal time of publication.

10th January 1840. Penny prepaid postage was introduced; formerly the recipient of a letter paid a not insignificant sum on its arrival. The new cheap system practically put an end to the real art of letter writing.

15th January 1779. David Garrick died at his house in the Adelphi. He was born on 19th February 1716 at an inn at Hereford. We may take him as the first representative of the modern successful actor, outstanding on the stage and in the brilliant society of his day. His business acumen enabled him to leave about £100,000.

16th January 1797. John Hetherington was arraigned and charged with a breach of the peace and inciting to riot, for wearing 'a tall structure having a shiny lustre, and calculated to frighten a timid people.' Women fainted, children screamed, and dogs yelped at the sight of it—an inauspicious first public appearance of the silk top-nat.

20th January 1265. Simon de Montfort and his barons, with the support of the common people (Henry III being safely locked up), called a parliament. In addition to the knights, Simon called two citizens from each borough. This occasion is regarded as the foundation of our House of Commons, and is undoubtedly our January epoch-maker.

20th January 1900. John Ruskin died at Coniston. He was born in Brunswick Square, London, on 8th February 1819. To some he is a symbol of the intellectual and spiritual conflicts of our age. Social reformer, critic, and even artist, we see him, a Canute-like figure, gradually swamped by the terrific tide of the nineteenth century. His wild and sometimes glorious splashings are still remembered as we ourselves are in turn swamped by the even heavier seas of our own times.

28th January 1807. Pall Mall—from St. James's Palace to Cockspur Street —twinkled as the row of gas lamps were lit. It was the first street in the world to be illumined by gas. The persistence of a German, Herr Winser, had overcome almost general mocking opposition to the project—most people believed that the pipes carrying the gas would get so hot as to cause damage by fire.

29th January 1728. The Beggar's Opera, by John Gay, was first performed at Lincoln's-Inn Fields theatre (manager Mr. Rich), having previously been refused by Colley Cibber of Drury Lane. The audience was uninterested up to the point when Polly (Lavinia Fenton) sang:

> For on the rope that hangs my dear
> Depends poor Polly's life . . .

From that moment success was assured, and we can consider that it is our January record-maker, for the opera has since been played many times—a famous run being that of Sir Nigel Playfair's production from 5th June 1920 to 17th December 1923.

25th January 1888. It would be a blot on any English almanac to omit a word or two about Edward Lear who died at San Remo on this day. Remembered as an inspired genius of poetic nonsense, he was in addition a most skilful draughtsman of birds, as well as a subtle painter of the landscapes in Italy, Greece, Albania, and Corsica. Ill health and a sad disposition caused him to spend most of his life wandering round these countries. He was born at Holloway on 12th May 1812.

30th January 1649. King Charles I was beheaded. In the popular mind he soon became regarded as a martyr and saint; even on the day of his burial snow fell and the black pall was turned to white—a sign of his innocence. He died when the age of miracle-working had passed, though handkerchiefs dipped in his blood did cure any illness.

On the Restoration the anniversary of his death was kept by the Church. Special prayers for the occasion were not removed from the prayer book until 1859.

THE POET

In January the height of winter is reached, and so we may begin with the full majesty of James Thomson's description in *The Seasons*:

> For now, behold! the joyous Winter days,
> Frosty, succeed; and through the blue serene,
> For sight too fine, the ethereal nitre flies,
> Killing infectious damps, and the spent air
> Storing afresh with elemental life.
> Close crowds the shining atmosphere; and binds
> Our strengthened bodies in its cold embrace,
> Constringent; feeds, and animates our blood;
> Refines our spirits, through the new-strung nerves
> In swifter sallies darting to the brain—
> Where sits the soul, intense, collected, cool,

Bright as the skies, and as the season keen.
All nature feels the renovating force
Of Winter—only to the thoughtless eye
In ruin seen. . . .

     : . . Then appears
The various labour of the silent night:
Prone from the dripping eave, and dumb cascade,
Whose idle torrents only seem to roar,
The pendant icicle; the frost-work fair,
Where transient hues and fancied figures rise;
Wide-spouted o'er the hill, the frozen brook,
A livid tract, cold-gleaming on the morn;
The forest bent beneath the plumy wave;
And by the frost refined the whiter snow
Incrusted hard, and sounding to the tread
Of early shepherd, as he pensive seeks
His pining flock, or from the mountain top,
Pleased with the slippery surface, swift descends.

  On blithesome frolics bent, the youthful swains,
While every work of man is laid at rest,
Fond o'er the river crowd, in various sport
And revelry dissolved; where, mixing glad,
Happiest of all the train! the raptured boy
Lashes the whirling top.

After that it must be said that, though many poets describe the bitterness which may be in January, such as Sir Osbert Sitwell's icy

   Through his iron glades
   Rides Winter the Huntsman . . .,

few mention it by name.

Except for the odes and 'lines' written on New Year's Day there is little else.

These odes have little to do with the month, being mostly gifts of flattery, such as Thomas Carew's lines, opening:

   Look back, old Janus, and survey
   From Time's birth till this new-born day . . .

—the survey showing that there has never been a monarch quite like Charles I, to whom the poem is addressed.

Or Sir John Suckling's

> Awake, great sir, the sun shines here
> Gives all your subjects a New Year . . .

and so on.

Wassailing songs are due this month. As they are either doggerel or sham antique, they can be left out except for some rather imaginative verses by the Victorian, Robert Stephen Hawker:

> Waes-hael for knight and dame!
>   O merry be their dole!
> Drink-hael! in Jesu's name
>   We fill the tawny bowl;
> But cover down the curving crest,
> Mould of the Orient Lady's breast.
>
> Waes-hael! yet lift no lid:
>   Drain ye the reeds for wine.
> Drink-hael! the milk was hid
>   That soothed that Babe divine;
> Hush'd, as this hollow channel flows,
> He drew the balsam from the rose.

Snow poems could find their place here but they are not peculiar to January; the reader in search of them is reminded of Walter de la Mare, whose

> There blooms no bud in May
> Can for its white compare . . .

is but one of several of his landscapes dusted with 'frozen foam.'

Even more famous and often quoted are Robert Bridges's lines on London snow. But, more aptly for our need here, this poet has written on January itself:

> Cold is the winter day, misty and dark:
>   The sunless sky with faded gleams is rent:
> And patches of thin snow outlying, mark
>   The landscape with a drear disfigurement.
>
> The trees their mournful branches lift aloft:
>   The oak with knotty twigs is full of trust,
> With bud-thronged bough the cherry in the croft;
>   The chestnut holds her gluey knops upthrust.

18

No birds sing, but the starling chaps his bill
    And chatters mockingly; the newborn lambs
Within their strawbuilt fold beneath the hill
    Answer with plaintive cry their bleating dams.

Their voices melt in welcome dreams of spring,
    Green grass and leafy trees and sunny skies:
My fancy decks the woods, the thrushes sing,
    Meadows are gay, bees hum and scents arise.

And God the Maker doth my heart grow bold
    To praise for wintry works not understood,
Who all the worlds and ages doth behold,
    Evil and good as one, and all as good.

FEBRUARY  AQUARIUS

FEBRUARY, our second month, has twenty-eight days, except when the year can be divided by four. Then it is a leap year, having twenty-nine.

It is the other month added to the original Roman calendar by the rather fabulous Numa. He placed it after December, but in 452 B.C. the Decemvirs —unmythical magistrates—moved it to go between January and March.

The purpose of leap year is to tidy up the odd day that accumulates because the earth goes round the sun in $365\frac{1}{4}$ and not exactly 365 days. The name 'leap year' comes from the fact that in ordinary years a date that is on, shall we say, Monday in one year always falls on Tuesday the next. But in leap years it will jump to Wednesday after 28th February has passed.

The year 1824 was a leap year. The first of the month fell on a Sunday, and so there were five Sundays in February. This will not happen again until—well, I often meet people who can solve this kind of problem.

It was in February that St. Patrick met St. Bridget, just after he had cleared the snakes out of Ireland. She was in tears. There was a mutiny at her convent because the girls had claimed a right to propose marriage to their men, and had learned that this was forbidden. After a long and very Irish conversation St. Patrick conceded them the right to make a proposal once every leap year. Now it so happened that this very meeting happened on the 29th and Bridget at once proposed marriage. Regretfully and with some difficulty (for there was much in the conversation that I have not quoted) St. Patrick declined on account of his vows, but to ease the tense situation he promised Bridget a silken gown.

20

That is why girls can now propose in leap year and if not accepted claim a silken gown.

February is derived from the Februa, Roman ceremonies of purification, presided over by the god Februus.

Anglo-Saxons called it the month of Sprout-Kale.

To us it is the season when Lent, with its abstinence, begins, and growth, with its promise of abundance, becomes apparent.

Both are symbolized in that hellebore which now throws up its vigorous spikes from among battered leaves, opens its many-coloured, speckled flowers, and is called the Lenten rose.

THE WEATHER

> . . . came cold February, sitting
> In an old wagon, for he could not ride,
> Drawn of two fishes for the season fitting,
> Which through the flood before did softly slide
> And swim away . . .

So said Spenser, referring to the age-old connection between February and rain—'February fill-dike.' In fact, February is on the average a fairly dry month; what is embodied in the old saying is a request for a 'black or white' February—that is, rain or snow. Both are equally desirable to safeguard the farmer against spring droughts.

The month is usually a cold one, with some days giving a hint of spring. The normal temperature is just under 40° F.

The 7th to 14th February inclusive are the days of Buchan's first cold spell. On the 14th in 1766 the Rev. William Cole wrote in his diary: 'The most singular Appearance on the Trees, and the most beautiful I ever saw. Every Twig and Leaf of the Ever-greens were christalized and the Wind shaking them, the large Trees made a very odd and surprising noise. . . . What was as odd . . . Kites and Hawkes fell from the Trees and were carried into the House, their Wings and Feathers being so frozen that they could not gett off.'

Candlemas Day, the 2nd, is particularly connected with rhymes prophesying the future:

> If Candlemas-day be fair and bright,
> Winter will have another flight;
> But if Candlemas-day be clouds and rain
> Winter is gone and will not come again.

also:

> Candlemas come and gone
> The snow lies on a hot stone.

THE HEAVENS

At the beginning of the month the sun is still in the sign of Aquarius, but after the middle, passes into Pisces, the Fishes.

The days now lengthen rapidly; London daylight increases in length by over two and a quarter hours during the month.

FEASTS, FAIRS, AND FESTIVALS

1st February. St. Bridget.

This saint was an Ulster woman, who built herself a cell under an oak-tree. Later she founded several nunneries. She was quite good at miracles; for instance, once she multiplied some butter that was given to her and presented the proceeds to the poor.

She is better known as the St. Bride of London's church.

2nd February. The Purification of the Blessed Virgin Mary or Candlemas.

What could better replace the pagan processions bearing flaming torches in honour of Ceres than a feast of candles twinkling to commemorate 'a light to lighten the Gentiles . . .'? Thus this holy day was established in the fifth century. The whole church was lit by their flickering light and those on the altar were blessed. There were processions, too, in which each worshipper carried a candle or taper.

c   23

It was also traditional that the use of candles and tapers at vespers and litanies, which prevailed during the darkest winter days, ceased from now until the next All Hallows mass.

After the Reformation this feast of candles was regarded dubiously, especially so in Puritan times.

Two old names for the snowdrop, Mary's tapers and Candlemas bells, link the plant with this day.

Double and Single Snowdrops

3rd February. St. Blaise.

He was an Armenian bishop, who is now the patron saint of wool-combers and of those who suffer from troubles in the throat. Some say he is the former because he invented wool-combing, others because he was martyred in the fourth century by sharp combs which tore his flesh to pieces. His second patronage is due to his miraculous removal of a bone in a boy's throat while on the way to his death.

Processions and pageants were held in the wool towns on his feast. There are records of those held at Bury St. Edmunds in the eighteenth century, and of a septennial event held at Bradford in the nineteenth. Their degree of glory rather reflected the prosperity of the wool trade at the time; when trade was bad the saint was inclined to be neglected.

14th February. St. Valentine.

We are told that whereas Candlemas replaced the orgy of the torch processions in the pagan festivals, the tradition attached to St. Valentine is a relic of the drawing of lots for women which was part of the same rite.

Why this tradition has been attached to one of the fifty-two saints named Valentine is not known. Two of them seem to have been martyred on this day, and both are quite unsuited to the occasion. One was a Roman priest and physician martyred under Claudius the Goth in 269, and the other a man of chastity who was slain in 870. Possibly the accident of date caused the connection.

Although the theme remains constant, there are many variations in the customs. Drawing of lots among groups of young people continued in a light-hearted way. Each boy when he had drawn his Valentine gave her a gift. Another custom was that the first man seen by a woman on the day was her Valentine.

Later the written Valentine, sometimes an elaborate composition, came into use until this was replaced by a lace-edged, elaborately printed card sent by the new penny post, and produced by the new printing process of early Victorian days. Valentine presents were also given.

The printed Valentine has had a chequered career. Coming into use before the Christmas card, it nearly disappeared until a comparatively recent revival. It has evolved in two distinct forms. First there is the traditional delicately ornate card, bearing a tender and sentimental rhyme. This produced a reaction in the comic and crude Valentine, which, with the anonymity of the sender, is a comparatively recent development.

The other Valentine tradition is, in the old words, 'Birds chuse their mates, and couple, too, this day.'

20th February. St. Mildred.

During medieval times this English saint was immensely popular among the people. She was given a good start by being born the daughter of a saint, Ermenburga of Thanet. First Abbess of Minster in Thanet, her mortal remains were removed to Canterbury, where they proved to be efficacious in miracle working. Later they were transferred to Holland, and much later still brought back to Thanet; apparently their mystic power had departed by then.

23rd February. St. Milborough.

This saint was sister to St. Mildred, and is famed as the builder of the monastery at Wenlock in Shropshire. She had remarkable powers. For instance, a young man becoming enamoured of her and pressing his suit too strongly, she became nervous and fled from his attentions. But he pursued her. Having crossed the stream that flows down Corvedale she arranged that it should swell to a great size. This duly happened and so frightened the young man that he gave up the chase.

At her request wild geese left off feeding on her monastic lands.

Her grave was found in 1100. The soil possessed such curative properties that for a time the local doctors were put out of practice.

24th February. St. Matthias. Apostle.

This rather shadowy figure was chosen by lots drawn by the remaining eleven disciples to replace Judas Iscariot. Little has become associated with his name or festival, and the books of reference dismiss him with such phrases as 'the traditions of his after life are not consistent.'

THE SPORTSMAN

In England salmon fishing, with both rod and net, starts on the first of the month. Netting ends on 31st August, rod fishing on 31st October. In Scotland there is some variation in the dates according to the rivers. This sport of plutocrats opens when the fish have completed their spawning; the prime of the season is from a little later on until early summer. Salmon is one of the few fish caught in our fresh waters which are consumed as food (so far as the purse permits) by the English people. The Wye is said to be the longest salmon stream in England.

Coursing of hares (animals as opposed to mechanical devices) with greyhounds celebrates its great occasion during the month when the ties for the Waterloo Cup take place.

It is illegal to shoot or take pheasant and partridge after the first; shooting usually ends rather earlier.

By tradition the holders for the time being of the Football Association Cup return it to the association on 1st February. Millions now follow the progress of their favourite team (if it is still in the running) with an interest almost greater than in life itself.

THE NATURALIST

February—you can have a headline with all the moderation and authenticity of *The Times*: 'Crows Attack Sheep' (which they killed and ate, so cold was it) or you can have—as is more usual—a few of those soft, grey days when the naturalist feels, a little uneasily, that spring might be just round the corner. But generally one may contentedly accept the precocities of January as normal in February, and indeed the month has many events in its own right which habitually accept the hazards of further snow and ice.

Missel-thrush

Many as are the signs that stir the botanist, it is the ornithologist who must receive pride of place, which is only right and proper in St. Valentine's month. The increased activity of birds is audible; the great-tit now makes a screeching din, the missel-thrush sings more powerfully, the song-thrush more frequently; during the middle of the month the chaffinch and wren usually join the singers. Wood-pigeons murmur and the lark sings more and more as he finds in his ascending that the sun is a little nearer.

Great crested grebes will be performing their courting antics on the water and pairing; lapwings will be doing the same in the air; the rook, too, will be back at the rookery, conversationally tinkering about with his nest and displaying himself in courtship flights. Partridge pair, and rook, raven, heron, and missel-thrush may have got as far as egg-laying.

Bird movements begin, though when chiff-chaffs and blackcaps are reported they are usually birds that have wintered with us in the south-western counties.

In the southern counties or in mild weather animal life stirs. Frogs and newts may wake up; in some places the frog may even be spawning at the end of the month.   Toads, lizards, and snakes of all kinds may take an airing though they are not really on the move yet.   Moles come up from their deep winter tunnels, and fresh mole workings are seen again.

One of the most universal February flowers is coltsfoot, opening its yellow flowers on scaly stems before the leaves unfold.   It is a colonizer and lover of waste places, which it makes not only gay, but useful, for it is one of the first nectar-bearing flowers visited by bees.   The plant has a long, popular, and botanical history.   Its old country name was 'sons before fathers'; while its botanical name *Tussilago* comes from *tussis*, a cough—syrup of colts-foot and tobacco from the leaves were much used for bronchial troubles.

In the woods the green rosettes and earliest leaves of many plants are noticeable.   Celandine may be out, and where snowdrops are naturalized they will be flowering.

We shall notice the catkins on those trees that are formed before winter are loosening, but usually they do not scatter pollen until March.   But the little flowers of the yew-tree are quite often open on a fine day and a gust of wind will raise clouds of their yellow dust.   The crimson flowers of the wych-elm are also seen in February.   The pale greenish bells of *Daphne Laureola*, cluster-ing around the bases of the dark green leaves, may be found.   Where this rather local shrub grows one can play the old game of sniffing to see whether or not the flower is scented, for fragrance is a fugitive attribute of the plant.

A cold February and the garden looks very lifeless; even those flowers proper to the month, such as Lent lilies, look a sorry sight.   On the other hand, this is my list towards the end of a mild month such as we had in 1943 or 1949: Crocus, *Imperati, chrysanthus,* and *Sieberi,* with a few odd clumps of the common orange kind that always come out early; daffodils, the lovely *pallidus praecox* and the minute *asturiensis*; snowdrops, both single and double; hellebores, both Christmas and Lent roses in abundance; of shrubs: the mezereon or common daphne; the old golden cornel or cornelian cherry; the Chinese guelder rose called *Viburnum fragrans*; great yellow spikes among the dark green, spiny leaves on *Berberis japonica*; the little, scented *Sarcococca* or sweet box; rhododendrons such as *praecox*, and, of course, the winter-flowering heaths of which Springwood White is one of the most vigorous.   All these were flowering freely—and many more kinds were doing so in a more half-hearted way.

There does not seem to be much insect life in February, though the bee-keeper may be annoyed if his bees become too active. A few other dingy moths may appear—one is aptly named the Quaker.

But, remember, February can be nearly all real winter, and in some years little is seen of what I have told above.

ANNIVERSARIES, EPOCHS, AND RECORDS

5th February 1819. Perhaps this was the Friday on which died Cavanagh, greatest of fives players. 'It may be said,' wrote Hazlitt in commemorating him, 'that there are things of more importance than striking a ball against a wall—there are things indeed which make more noise and do as little good, such as making war and peace . . .'

7th February 1845. Mr. William Lloyd dashed the famous Portland vase to pieces. It was regarded as a treasure almost beyond price, and had been on show in the British Museum since 1810. When Mr. Lloyd was prosecuted and convicted a gentleman in court paid the fine. The vase was successfully mended by a Mr. Doubleday.

8th February 1750. England was shaken by her last great earthquake, so graphically described by many authors. Walpole tells how he was awakened believing someone to be under the bed lifting it up.

10th February. For no discernible reason the almanacker Chambers includes a note about umbrellas on this day. So why should not we also honour to-day the unknown inventor of this device, so invaluable in our climate?

11th February 1908. At the Royal Horticultural Society's show Messrs. Suttons exhibited 268 varieties of potato. This will suffice for our February record.

18th February 1478. George, Duke of Clarence, was by order of his brother Richard, Duke of Gloucester, drowned in a butt of malmsey. So we learnt in our kindergarten, and scientific historians are still unable to disprove the story. What is a butt? A cask holding 104 to 140 gallons. What is malmsey? A strong, sweet wine from Greece.

21st February 1740. Jethro Tull, born at Basildon, died at Prosperous Farm, Hungerford. To him we owe a revolution in farming practice, for he invented the method of sowing seed by drill (his machine was based on part of the sound-board of an organ), and as the crop grew hoeing to keep it clean. Trained as a lawyer, ill health made him take to farming, and after travelling abroad he settled down to a life of experiment, which finally triumphed over the malicious activities of the ignorant, ill health, and a farm on difficult, hungry land.

22nd February 1797. The French invaded Britain and successfully landed an armed force in South Wales. Episodes such as the victorious attack on one of their units by Jemima Nicholas armed only with a pitchfork and her tongue, combined with a retreat of the transporting ships, so disheartened our invaders that they soon surrendered.

23rd February. Two of the very few English practitioners of the arts to achieve fame outside their native country died on this day—the first, Sir Joshua Reynolds in 1792, and the second, Sir Edward Elgar, in 1934.

The end of the painter was typical of his calm and spacious art. After a year or two of gradually declining health he became ill for a month or two. 'I have,' he said, 'been fortunate in long good health and constant success, and I ought not to complain. I know that all things on earth must have an end.' We are told that 'with those simple words of resignation he expired without pain in his sixty-ninth year.'

Sir Edward Elgar, Master of the King's Musick, died near Worcester, in which county he was born on 2nd June 1857. International fame and honour, practically unknown to an English musician since Purcell's day, came to him after *The Dream of Gerontius*. Yet his finest music—at times touched with a magnificent, noisy grandeur in tune with the feelings of the common people, at others with the moody feeling of storms and uneasy calms in the Welsh border hills, or perhaps even more often, with the stirrings and sounds that surround quiet streams flowing through the green midland orchard lands— is too English in its allusions and sentiment to be within the comprehension of our modern cosmopolitan suburbia.

25th February 1723. Sir Christopher Wren died. He was a parson's son born at East Knoyle, Wiltshire, on 20th October 1632. At Oxford he was distinguished as a mathematician and became an astronomer. Charles II asked him to prepare plans to remodel the crumbling old cathedral of St. Paul's and, as far as he was able, convert its Gothic rudeness into the fashionable Roman manner. Just after, the cathedral and most of the city were burned down, and Wren was given an opportunity of starting afresh such as can have been offered to few men. Naturally, business men prevented his doing the whole job as he wished, but St. Paul's Cathedral and many other churches and public buildings (not a few of which have been in their turn burnt out by fire dropped from the air) stand as Wren's monument. He is also a memorial to changing taste; to-day we deplore the Victorians, who, we must remember, in their turn were very dubious about Wren and regarded his age as a period of deplorable taste.

THE POET

The poetry of February is rather a mixed lot. The weather may give us an ice-bound land, or we may find in it the pause before the coming of spring described by Laurence Binyon:

> Peacefully fresh, O February morn,
> Thy winds come to me. . . .

Or we may see winter depart, as did John Clare:

> The hedgehog, from his hollow root,
> Sees the wood-moss clear of snow,
> And hunts the hedge for fallen fruit—
> Crab, hip, and winter-bitten sloe;
> But often check'd by sudden fears,
> As shepherd-dog his haunt espies,
> He rolls up in a ball of spears,
> And all his barking rage defies.

As every one knows, Wordsworth celebrated February as the month of one of his favourite flowers, the lesser celandine.

On looking at the contents of the collected works of Tennyson I certainly found a title *The Third of February 1852*, and expected to find one of his perfect descriptive passages, but instead I read:

> The niggard throats of Manchester may bawl
> What England was, shall her true sons forget?
> We are not cotton-spinners all,
> But some love England and her honour yet.

So having brought the poets down to a more worldly state of mind we come to that particular feature of February verse, the Valentine.

Apart from the myriad superb but anonymous poets of the lacy cards, the number from which to choose a representative selection is vast.

Lord Macaulay, for example, is seen in one of his less didactic moods in his *Valentine*:

> Hail, day of music, day of love,
> On earth below, in air above.
> In air the turtle fondly moans,
> The linnet pipes in joyful tones;
> On earth the postman toils along,
> Bent double by huge bales of song,
> Where, rich with many a gorgeous dye,
> Blazes all Cupid's heraldry—
> Myrtles and roses, doves and sparrows,
> Love-knots and altars, lamps and arrows.
> What nymph without wild hopes and fears
> The double rap this morning hears?
> Unnumbered lasses, young and fair,
> From Bethnal Green to Belgrave Square,
> With cheeks high-flushed, and hearts loud beating,
> Await the tender annual greeting.
> The loveliest lass of all is mine—
> Good morrow to my Valentine! . . .

and so on for another thirty-five lines until we arrive triumphantly at the portico of St. George's, Hanover Square, for a society wedding.

Or we have Charles Stuart Calverley, with typical Victorian ingenuity:

> Ere the morn the east has crimsoned,
> When the stars are twinkling there
> (As they did in Watts's Hymns, and
> Made him wonder what they were),

When the forest nymphs are beading
  Fern and flower with silvery dew—
My infallible proceeding
  Is to wake and think of you.

Going back to the days of real ballads Charles Dibdin gives us a melancholy Valentine:

O lovely day! ah me! the while
  How hard, alas! to see
That nature should so sweetly smile
  On all the world but me!
Hark the gay tenants of the air,
  How gratefully they sing!
And hail by instinct, as they pair,
  The harbinger of spring!

Still earlier, we approach perfection in Lancelot Andrewes, whose life nearly spanned the reigns of Elizabeth and James I:

Come, be my Valentine!
I 'll gather eglantine,
Cowslips and sops-in-wine,
  With fragrant roses.
Down by thy Phillis sit,
She will white lilies get,
And daffadillies fit
  To make thee posies.

I have a milk-white lamb,
New taken from the dam,
It comes where'er I am
  When I call 'Willy':
I have a wanton kid
Under my apron hid,
A colt that ne'er was rid,
  A pretty filly.

I bear in sign of love
A sparrow in my glove,
And in my breast a dove,
  This shall all be thine:

> Besides of sheep a flock,
> Which yieldeth many a lock,
> And this shall be thy stock:
> Come, be my Valentine!

And finally Wilfred Scawen Blunt, perhaps an Elizabethan in spirit, born into the great days of Victoria and her successors, gave us this most English of St. Valentine's Days:

> To-day, all day, I rode upon the down,
> With hounds and horsemen, a brave company.
> On this side in its glory lay the sea,
> On that the Sussex weald, a sea of brown.
> The wind was light, and brightly the sun shone,
> And still we gallop'd on from gorse to gorse:
> And once when check'd, a thrush sang, and my horse
> Prick'd his quick ears as to a sound unknown.
> I knew the spring was come. I knew it even
> Better than all by this, that through my chase
> In bush and stone and hill and sea and heaven
> I seem'd to see and follow still your face.
> Your face my quarry was. For it I rode,
> My horse a thing of wings, myself a god.

MARCH  PISCES

MARCH has thirty-one days. As has been told, Romulus placed it first in his calendar, and until 1752 it closed and opened our own legal year. Now it is our third month, named after Martius, god of war.

The Anglo-Saxons called it Hlydmonath, the loud (or stormy) month, and Lenctenmonath, month of lengthening days.

These names graphically describe the two outstanding qualities of a month which blusters its way through from a wintry beginning to an end when we may unexpectedly find ourselves in spring; as the old saying has it, March borrows his last three days from April.

It is a month of planting and propagation. Potatoes are put in the ground (traditionally on Good Friday) and fruit trees are grafted.

There is one dreadful happening in our history that occurred in March which it is salutary to recall—in 1665 London first found itself in the grip of the plague. Let us remember too those men and women who faced almost certain death, and bravely remained in the plague spots—not London alone —to maintain organization, law, and order.

As every one knows, March is the month of wild daffodils and mad hares, to which I would add the cultivated crocus. And in the days when epicures' calendars were practical and reliable documents, duckling came into season.

THE WEATHER

Records of this, the first of the spring months, justify its traditions. It has been said (by a scientist) to show 'a hasty panorama of all the seasons.' During the twentieth century it has achieved both a temperature falling below

35

zero, and the warmth of a hot summer day, when the thermometer rose to 77° F. Normal temperature is about 41° F.

Some of the worst blizzards we have suffered were in March. In 1667 Evelyn wrote in his diary on the 6th: 'Great frosts, snow, and winds, prodigious at the vernal equinox; indeed, it has been a year of prodigies in the nation, plague, war, fire, rains, tempest, and comet.'

Statistics show it to be both one of our windiest and driest months—hence the need for a February to fill the dikes.

THE HEAVENS

Until the 20th or 21st the sun remains in Pisces, then moves into Aries, the Ram.

At the time it moves from one to another occurs the vernal equinox. Day and night are equal all over the world. The sun rises and sets due east and west, at very nearly 6 a.m. and 6 p.m.

FEASTS, FAIRS, AND FESTIVALS

1st March. St. David.

The patron of Wales. He was son of Xantu, Prince of Cardiganshire. The legend that he first achieved fame at a synod held in 519 at Brevy in Cardiganshire, where by his eloquence, learning, and skill at miracle working he was able to confound the view held by Pelagius that there was no taint of Adam in man is now discredited.

He founded twelve monasteries. His diet consisted of bread and vegetables, particularly leeks which he found sustaining; hence this plant is carried by Welshmen as a symbol on this day. He drank only milk and water.

On his death St. Kentigern saw David's soul being borne by angels to heaven.

His father was not married to his mother.

The daffodil is also associated with this saint and the day. Growing wild in Wales and the Welsh marshes, it is said to open its blossoms on 1st March.

2nd March.   St. Chad.

This saint died in 673, having founded and been the first bishop of the see of Lichfield. He became rather popular as a patron of churches and establishments.

Just before and at his death he was seen attended by musical angels.

17th March.   St. Patrick.

Born, some say, in Scotland, he was carried as a slave to Ireland.   Later he travelled in Europe.   Next Pope Celestine gave him an apostolic mission to convert the Irish to Christianity.   This he succeeded in doing, displaying great enthusiasm and outstanding administrative ability.   He was helped, too, by the abundance of miracles that he was able to work—not least of which was the elimination of all venomous beasts from the country.

Not unnaturally his adopted countrymen acclaimed him as their patron saint.   He chose the shamrock as an emblem in explaining the Trinity to the Irish people.

There are those who contend that he was a Welshman born at Aberllychwr in Pembrokeshire.   He died on this day about 461.

20th March.   St. Edward.   King of the West Saxons.

In 978 this Edward, having been chosen king by the Witan, was set upon and murdered when nearing Corfe Castle. (His riderless horse can still be heard in that part of Dorset.)   His stepmother was responsible as she wished her son Ethelred to rule.

The murderers thought that they had successfully hidden the body, but before long miracles began to happen at the spot which they had chosen.   A search followed, and the corpse was found, still uncorrupted.

He became a popular hero, and was canonized by the people.

25th March.   Annunciation of the Blessed Virgin Mary or Lady Day.

Before the Reformation this feast dedicated to Our Lady was of great consequence.   To-day it is best known as the first quarter-day of the year.

From the twelfth century until 1752 it was the first day of the legal year, though popular opinion held to the 1st January.

Traditionally it was this day that Christ was crucified. Therefore a year of ill luck should follow if Easter Day or Good Friday (there is some doubt which) falls on the 25th.

The Tichborne Dole is given every Lady Day in compliance with the dying wish of Lady Mabella Tichborne, who lived during the reign of Henry I. Her mean husband said that she might leave to the poor a gift of flour from the area of land around which she could walk before a faggot burned out. Too weak to walk she crawled around twenty-three acres. The plot is still known as The Crawls, and the flour from it blessed and given away at the door of the village church. The beneficiaries are the villagers of Tichborne and Cheriton in Hampshire.

In the old-style calendar Lady Day fell on what is now 6th April.

31st March. Oranges and Lemons.

The attendants of Clement's Inn used on this day to visit the residents and give to them oranges and lemons. They were rewarded with a gift.

It was revived in a new form. The children of the parish visited the church of St. Clement Danes, and while the bells rang out the old tune, were given oranges and lemons presented by the Danish colony in London, whose church it has been for many generations. The bells whose song is famed in nursery rhyme were destroyed in an air-raid.

THE SPORTSMAN

With the decreasing possibility of hard frost and deep snow the sportsman now enters a period when many events proper to winter end, while others move towards a climax, and have added to them the joys peculiar to spring and early summer. The month usually includes two of our most popular events, known simply as the Boat Race and the National.

But let us deal with these many important matters in some sort of order.

First, fishing, since this touches both democracy and the modest plutocrat during the month, for trout fishing opens and coarse fishing ends.

The trout season begins on the 1st, though this day varies in some places. Coarse fishing in fresh waters ends on the 14th; after that date there is a close period until 16th June.

Fishing for char, a large fresh-water member of the salmon family, which became marooned in our deepest and coldest lakes when the waters receded, also comes into season on the 1st—with local variations. In Windermere char is taken seriously as an edible fish and netted; potted Windermere char is, we are told, a local delicacy.

The man with the gun must be careful what he shoots. After 1st March it is an offence under the Wild Birds Act to shoot wild duck (mallard or teal), plover, snipe, and nominally wood-pigeon. On the same day begins the close time for quail and land-rail; also it is illegal to sell or have for sale for human consumption an egg of the common plover or lapwing.

On the other hand, diaries still inform us that the season for bustard begins on the 2nd; once this big and very edible bird bred here, and droves wandered over Salisbury Plain and the Yorkshire wolds. It is now only an occasional winter visitor.

March is the month proper to the hare. This animal is so destructive that the Ground Game Act gives farmers an inalienable right to kill it at any time of the year except on Sundays or Christmas Day. It is, however, protected to some extent, and has the honour of being hunted, apart from coursing, and in three ways—by packs of beagles, basset-hounds, and harriers. Usually a green uniform is common to all these hunts. 'Merry beagles,' small, rather short-legged hounds, and basset-hounds, also low-built animals with long, drooping ears, are followed on foot. Harriers are rather light but long-legged hounds and lead a mounted field.

On Exmoor the hunting of hinds ends in early March; that of young stags begins in the last weeks. In the north stalking of hinds ends with the month.

The last days of the month give racegoers famous events both on the flat and in steeplechasing. The flat-racing season starts in the week that includes quarter-day, the 25th; should that be Easter week then a week earlier. In the first week of the flat-racing season the Grand National Steeplechase is run. Apart from the crowds visiting the course by every means of travel, from luxury aircraft to hitch-hiking, a few millions follow it who know nothing of racing, for it has become a national institution. To these people Becher's Brook and the Canal Turn are names familiar as the Tower of London and Wormwood Scrubs. To them the form of their fancied choice and state of the going are of more immediate concern than war or peace. The race was founded in 1842. On all but four occasions it has been run at Aintree, Liverpool's otherwise undistinguished suburb. The length is 'about [*sic*] 4 miles 856 yards.' There are thirty jumps.

The first big meeting of the flat-racing season is held in the last days of the month on the 'ratepayer's racecourse,' at Carholme, Lincoln. The big race is the Lincolnshire Handicap. This was first run on a different course in August 1849. The winner was Lord Exeter's Midia—who ran in two other events on the same day.

One of our other national institutions of sport, the Boat Race (no need to say which), is also usually rowed at the end of March or sometimes in early April. The traditional date is the Saturday before Good Friday or as near as the tide permits. As I think every one must know it is rowed between eights from Oxford and Cambridge. The course is from Putney to Mortlake, passing many familiar points—a distance of four and a quarter miles. The race was first rowed in 1820—apparently at first in a rather casual way as no proper records were kept until 1836. In Edwardian times, we read, it could 'hardly be called a society function, though it is an affair of the greatest general interest.' And of general interest it certainly remains.

Finally at the end of March the badminton season closes.

One famous anniversary must be recalled, the first final of the Football Association Cup played on 16th March 1872. Some two thousand spectators were present. The finalists, the Wanderers, a team of ex-public school and university players, beat the Royal Engineers by one goal to none. All were amateurs. There was heavy betting on the result.

THE NATURALIST

Dark though the sky may be as storms pass and whiten the ground with falls of snow, there can be no doubt as March moves forward that growth is beginning to gain a vast and increasing momentum urged on by the mounting sun.

It is in the woods that we see most signs of this. The canopy of branches traps radiation of the accumulated day's heat from the earth during cold, clear nights, so that woodland soil becomes warm earlier than that in the open. Most of the woodland herbs, too, have to get their flowering finished before the leafing of the trees cuts the sunshine off from the forest floor. Perhaps for this reason many woodland herbs develop their leafy systems in very early spring before they flower. This is so with both Wordsworth's lesser celandine and wood anemone, which both flower freely and carpet open woods in March. Celandine attracts geneticists as well as poets, for

Wood Anemones (wild and cultivated)

there are two forms. One has none of those little tubers (well known to many tidy gardeners) and increases by means of seed. The other bears tubers in its leaf axils, and is propagated by them, for it produces little fertile seed.

Our wood anemone is found growing over a wide area of the northern hemisphere. It is surely one of our loveliest flowers, formed by a ring of large sepals which are coloured many shades, from white to pinks and blues, instead of the usual green. It is interesting to collect the different and always lovely forms that can be found. Another very common plant which

breaks away from both the usual yellows and blues of early spring and the habit of early leafing is dog's mercury—though the greenish flower-spikes look more leaf-like than floral. The god Mercury discovered its medicinal properties which mortals have now long forgotten. This abundant but uninteresting looking herb is related to our own spurges, and the weird euphorbias of other lands. Another striking exception to our spring rules is toothwort, which may now be found in flower under hazel-trees, upon whose roots it lives. This obviates the need to grow its own green leaves. The flowers, in a heavy architecturally designed spike, are a strange colour, usually not very accurately described as 'flesh.' They soon turn a sombre, purplish brown, and are handsome as decorations. In March, too, flowers another architectural beauty, the stinking hellebore or setterwort, another all-green plant. So far as I am aware it is quite innocuous in spite of its name.

Many trees, mostly catkin bearers, flower now. Unlike most herbs they do so before their leaves appear, on bare twigs. In the woods wych-elm, and in the hedgerows field-elm, will still probably be flowering. Their large-winged green fruit develop in a matter of days as soon as fertilization has taken place. In some years this makes the elms look prematurely leaved. Gayest of all are several kinds of shrubby osiers, willows, or sallows. The male bushes bear golden, pollen-bearing catkins, and the female more modest silvery ones—golden palm and pussy-willow. Both are covered with bees on mild days.

The alder, too, is often profusely catkined—long, pollen-bearing ones and little cone-like female flowers that become woody. In winter they open and the seed showers down and often floats to its destination. A fine old catkined alder, lit by the sun, overhanging a dark pool, is a lovely sight in its subtle March colourings of grey and pinkish browns.

Other trees bearing catkins now are our little native poplar, the aspen, larches (celebrated by Tennyson, abhorred by Wordsworth), and, where it grows in the eastern counties, hornbeam—looking rather odd, this, rather like a betasselled beech. Other poplars are also flowering. Undoubtedly the most handsome is our native black (called birch-leaved) poplar in its male form. This tree was once much planted along streams in flat park-land. Its heavy, black, open branches become covered with long crimson tassels. It is a brilliant and rather uncommon sight. Old trees grow top-heavy, and the branches fall apart and break up. They are eventually removed by energetic clearers of watercourses, and to-day nobody thinks to replant them—they are quite useless trees, only beautiful.

Two foreigners also bear catkins now—the Lombardy and balsam poplars. Both are undistinguished in bloom and foliage, but the first makes up for it with a spire-like shape, and the second with fragrance as the leaves unfold.

In the hedgerows blackthorn will be showing very white against the dark plough, and in orchards, damson—early to flower and late to fruit.

So much for the trees. Of herbs in open places the coltsfoot will still be prominent, while dandelions and daisies are opening their long season.

Stream and marsh flowers are mostly late bloomers, but surprisingly the marsh marigold starts now.

You may find other flowers, specially if the season has been mild. Those irrepressibles, chickweed and groundsel, are sure to be busy; ground-ivy (pretty general), a few dog violets, and wild pansies; the smaller speedwells and white deadnettle are sure to be found; Bentham and Hooker rightly describe them as 'Fl. the whole season.'

Suburbia becomes gay. Crocuses, purple, white, and orange, cover the ground. These continental and Asiatic visitors have been with us so long that we can almost regard them as natives. They are joined by the clear pink blossoms on the angular, open-branched almond-tree. This was brought here, probably from Algeria, early in the sixteenth century. Unlike the crocus it has not become naturalized and would soon disappear if it were not continually propagated and planted by gardeners. Another recent arrival has also become ubiquitous—the 'purple prunus,' known by nurserymen as *Prunus pissardii*. It was named after a Monsieur Pissart, gardener to the Shah of Persia, from whence it was brought to Europe at the end of last century. It is not considered to be in the best taste now; indeed, the cherry-plum or myrobalan, of which it is a purple or red-leafed form, is really more attractive, and in some years carries good crops of delicious little fruit. This is also found flowering in orchards and hedges.

So much for some of the more obvious excitements that greet the botanist. Bird-watchers are kept equally busy. Robins, blackbirds, hedge-sparrows, and thrushes are busy nesting. Blackbirds and chaffinches are two of the many birds now coming into full song. The great drumming contest gets well under way. It is, of course, between the supporters of different theories explaining the peculiar mechanical-sounding noises made by the greater spotted woodpecker as he clings to a tree and the snipe as he swoops through the air.

Migration becomes an important object of study as the spring movements of birds increase. Most welcome are our own early arrivals. March brings the wheatear. Some places will see chiff-chaffs at the end of the month, and rather fewer flocks of yellow wagtails. Possible arrivals are willow-wrens and sand-martins. Aristocratic geese and many of the ducks leave us; redwing and brambling move to the north. Puffins cease their wanderings and collect in crowds at their breeding places. At this season of the year they grow their fancy noses, which disappear in the autumn. Most seaside visitors imagine this decoration to be a permanency.

The lighter sleepers awake. Fine days bring out queen wasps. The boom of a queen bumble-bee as she starts her energetic year will take the mind forward to hot summer afternoons when the only sound seems to be a murmur of bees' wings. Honey-bees are, of course, out on every fine day searching crocus and sallows.

Both kinds of squirrel will be finishing their nest (or drey) building in the tops of trees. Badgers are spring-cleaning, turning out the bedding that has kept them warm during the winter and preparing new chambers in their deep sets, which they line with fern and grass ready to receive a new generation of 'earth pigs.'

Most kinds of bat leave their belfries and crevices and take a flight soon after the middle of the month. Lizards awake from their sound sleep and pair. Grass snakes may be out on a fine day. Toads will start their wanderings, and the more active frog may already have started breeding and spawning.

March in tradition and fact is the month when hares go mad—the buck cavorts and plays wild antics as he pursues the doe. The urge of spring makes the peaceful mole ferocious and quarrelsome. Both he and the little shrew will now fight their own kind to the death.

Of our larger animals March is a usual month for cubs to be born to foxes and whelps to otters. The stags of red deer drop their horns.

In the fish world miller's thumb, perch, and pike are spawning—the earliest fish to do so.

A small tortoise-shell butterfly, distracting the attention of the congregation as it flaps in the sunshine on a church window, is often the first reminder of the year that the supremacy of drab moths has ended. The husbands of those apterous, crawling females are soon forgotten when we see the first tortoise-shells, brimstones, and peacocks—three gay butterflies that hibernate so that they can begin the breeding season early. A few cabbage whites usually appear, as well as some slightly gayer moths, such as the yellow under-wing. Manuals inform collectors that towards the end of the month they may start sugaring and visiting catkined sallows with a lantern, but warn them that their yields may be meagre. On the other hand, hibernating larvae are getting active, and butterfly breeders may find a good number of caterpillars.

March ends and merges into April. During its weeks the tempo of growth has speeded enormously; 'early spring' of the text-books has changed to 'spring.'

ANNIVERSARIES, EPOCHS, AND RECORDS

1st March 1711. The *Spectator* was first issued. Addison and Steele were responsible for this, the forerunner of many subsequent periodicals. Its object was 'to bring philosophy out of closets and libraries, schools and colleges to dwell in clubs and assemblies, at the tea-tables, and at coffee-houses.'

2nd March 1791. John Wesley died. He was born in 1703. It is, perhaps, in accordance with the English character that this exponent of nonconformity with the rules of the established Church of England and the administrator who built up the powerful Methodist organization recruited from the new, rising class of shopkeepers and tradesmen, was himself of aristocratic lineage and educated at Charterhouse and Christ Church, Oxford. His capacity as preacher, controversialist, and organizer of the middle classes was matched by his enormous energy. He preached about 800 sermons in the year, the first often at five o'clock in the morning.

3rd March 1703. Robert Hooke, who was born in the Isle of Wight in 1635, died. He was long regarded as an ingenious old gentleman who was rather querulous, particularly about his grievance over Sir Isaac Newton's claims to some of his own discoveries. To-day, however, we are able to include him as probably the greatest inventive genius of scientific instruments that the world has ever known. If he had been a better mathematician he might have outshone Sir Isaac as a natural philosopher. However, as he invented (among other things) the anchor escapement used in clocks, probably also the balance wheel still found in all watches, most of our fundamental meteorological instruments, telescopic sights, numerous microscopic devices (he discovered the cellular structure of plants), the iris diaphragm and the universal joint, we may regard him as our epoch-maker.

20th March 1727. Sir Isaac Newton died. He was born on Christmas Day 1642. We recall him as an Englishman who had 'an unrivalled genius for mathematical speculation.' His work on the differential calculus, light, and gravitation must have profoundly affected the course of humanity. His unique mind was devoted to numerous undertakings down to the management of the Royal Mint. Deeply and unquestioningly a believer in the Church, just before death he likened his life to a boy playing on the sea-shore and picking up a few shells.

27th March 1899. The first wireless telegraphy signal was transmitted over-sea—from the South Foreland lighthouse to Wimereux in France, some thirty miles. The sender was Marconi, and his first message was one of congratulation to the French scientist Édouard Branly, whose researches had helped him.

29th March 1834. John Mytton, squire of Halston, Shropshire, died from delirium tremens in his thirty-eighth year. 'His princely munificence and eccentric gaieties obtained him great notoriety in the sporting and gay circles, both in England and the Continent.' He had separated fighting dogs by picking up one with his teeth, jumped horse and trap over a hedge, set himself on fire to cure his hiccups, and ridden into a dining-room full of his guests on the back of a bear. Undoubtedly he is a suitable record-breaker in the month of the hare.

30th March 1837. John Constable, R.A., died. Born at East Bergholt in the Stour valley of Suffolk, the son of a miller, he was insular and almost parochial in his life and painting. Yet his pictures of the unidealized landscape—clouds blowing across the sky, the greens and golds of fields and woods, the red of plough, the yellow of beaches—seen as the sun shone on them (perhaps fitfully)—roused enthusiasm in France long before most of his fellow country-men realized that here was one of our few great painters. He died suddenly, the paint still wet on a picture, with a studio full of unsold work. Happily he had some private means, otherwise he might have become just another portrait painter.

THE POET

Our earliest poets do not seem much interested in March. Its poetical symbolism is given in the lines from Chaucer:

> The month in which the world began
> That naméd March, when God first makéd man.

March winds are more often the subject of doggerel than of poetry, while the threatening reference to the Ides of March in *Julius Caesar* have more to do with the plot of that play than with the month. Shakespeare has, of course,

> . . . daffodils,
> That come before the swallow dares, and take
> The winds of March with beauty.

Later poets have made up for the omissions of their predecessors. The breezy and sometimes storm-clouded landscape with touches of spring in the detailed foreground has often been described, as in the lines written at Lolham Briggs by John Clare:

> Though o'er the darksome northern hill
>   Old ambush'd winter frowning flies,
> And faintly drifts his threatenings still
>   In snowy sleet and blackening skies;
>   Yet where the willow leaning lies
> And shields beneath the budding flower,
>   Where banks to break the wind arise,
> 'Tis sweet to sit and spend an hour.

> Though floods of winter bustling fall
>   Adown the arches bleak and blea,
> Though snow-storms clothe the mossy wall,
>   And hourly whiten o'er the lea;
>   Yet when from the clouds the sun is free
> And warns the learning bird to sing,
>   'Neath sloping bank and sheltering tree
> 'Tis sweet to watch the creeping spring.

> Here 'neath the shelving bank's retreat
>   The horse-blob swells its golden ball;
> Nor fear the lady-smocks to meet
>   The snows that round their blossoms fall:
>   Here by the arch's ancient wall
> The antique eldern buds anew;
>   Again the bulrush sprouting tall
> The water wrinkles, rippling through.

> The stirtling peewits, as they pass,
>   Scream joyous whizzing overhead,
> Right glad the fields and meadow grass
>   Will quickly hide their careless shed:
>   The rooks, where yonder witchens spread,
> Quawk clamorous to the spring's approach;
>   Here silent, from its watery bed,
> To hail its coming, leaps the roach.

Kingfisher

Tennyson must be quoted, if only to raise again the problem of the 'sea-blue bird':

> When rosy plumelets tuft the larch,
>   And rarely pipes the mounted thrush;
>   Or underneath the barren bush
> Flits by the sea-blue bird of March.

And Gerard Manley Hopkins:

> March-bloom, like on mealed-with-yellow sallows.

49

A. E. Housman's imagery of the missel-thrush, that bird of March, must be recalled:

> . . . braver notes the storm-cock sings
> To start the rusted wheel of things. . . .

Then there is William Morris's *The Message of the March Wind*:

> Fair now is the spring-tide, now earth lies beholding
> With the eyes of a lover, the face of the sun;
> Long lasteth the daylight, and hope is enfolding
> The green-growing acres with increase begun.
>
> .   .   .   .   .
>
> There is wind in the twilight; in the white road before us
> The straw from the ox-yard is blowing about;
> The moon's rim is rising, a star glitters o'er us,
> And the vane on the spire-top is swinging in doubt.

It goes on a good deal longer until we learn that the message to be delivered is an attack on Victorian industry.

Quite recently we have had Miss Sackville-West's picture:

> Shall I count March in Winter? yes, in this
> Dear northern island where the sun's late kiss
> Comes not till middle April.   We believe
> Too readily in pledges that deceive.
> In one day's promise of a warming air,
> In one day's painting by a stronger sun
> That on a sudden with a flying flare
> Deepens the shadows underneath the arch
> And touches all the tips to buds where none
> Yesterday showed, and sweeps a generous brush
> Across plantations of the ignoble larch,
> Across the lovelier copse
> With undefinable but certain flush
> Lingering on the catkins and the tops
> Of hazel and the sticky chestnut, when
> The small brown things are blown across the ground
> Between the fallen twigs and stubs and stones,
> —A leaf, a mouse, a wren?—
> All in a hurry in the wind of March.

Then what could be better to end March and welcome April than Miss Eleanor Farjeon's:

> March, blow by
> With your stormy grey eye!
> April, run in
> With your pear blossom skin!
> The catkin is shaking
> A powder of gold
> The daisy is breaking
> A way through the mould,
> The chaffinch is taking
> Her morsel of moss,
> The wind is making
> The rookery toss
> March, goodbye
> To your stormy grey eye!
> April, begin
> With the bloom on your chin!

APRIL

ARIES

APRIL has thirty days and is the fourth month of our year. Some say that the name comes from Latin, *aperire*, to open—'the womb of nature opens with young life.'

Anglo-Saxons certainly linked the month with a deity. They called it Easturmonath, in honour of Eastre, goddess of the east and rising sun.

In our islands it is the gardening month. If on a fine April evening we look from the windows of a railway carriage as the train winds along one of those high embankments which so often span our dense suburbs, there is displayed below a scene of vast industry in the myriad gardens within sight. On Saturday nights the pubs are full of very tired men whose talk is of gardening, for, excepting the Cup Final, football is on the way to eclipse.

As for the rest of April, it has all been said long ago by our poets—except that it is the month when crab comes into season.

THE WEATHER

We learn from statistics that during Victorian days April did not behave according to tradition. Instead of being changeable and showery it was more often than otherwise fine and dry. Perhaps it was the same in Evelyn's time, for he wrote of April 1681: 'But one shower of rain all this month.' During the nineteenth century there were some exceptionally warm spells, temperatures of 80° F. being reached.

Our own scientific century has, however, provided weather more in accordance with the poetic and story-book tradition. The weather has generally been both wetter and colder.

The 11th to 14th April comprise Buchan's second cold spell. Before he was discovered by the newspapers it was called blackthorn winter. A number of bad snowstorms and severe frosts have happened during the month, even after Easter has passed.

The normal temperature is about 45° F.

A number of old sayings agree that thunder in April ensures good crops:

> When April blows his horn
> 'Tis good for hay and corn.

THE HEAVENS

The sun remains in Aries for the first three weeks of the month and then climbs into the sign of Taurus, the Bull. Days are now longer than nights.

Some years there is a shower of falling stars between the 20th and 22nd.

Under the original Summer Time Act of 1925 the clocks were put forward in April to give us Mr. Willett's Summer Time. Now the date is variable.

FEASTS, FAIRS, AND FESTIVALS

1st April. All Fools' Day.

The old rhyme says of this world-wide custom:

> The first of April, some do say,
> Is set apart for All Fools' Day;
> But why the people call it so
> Nor I nor they themselves do know.

That seems to sum up the knowledge of our scholars and anthropologists. They say it is a very ancient and almost world-wide celebration of Everyman —the fool who is easily trapped into making a silly mistake, the eternal prey of the smart and cunning.

In these islands the essential of the ritual is that between midnight on the last day of March and noon on the 1st of April the victims must be duped into taking some positive action for no real reason, and will so find themselves in a laughable situation. For example, at the end of March in 1860 many Londoners received a fine, gilt-edged invitation card inviting them to attend the Annual Washing of the White Lions at the Tower of London on Sunday, 1st April. Full instructions were given as to the arrangements for the arrival of carriages, and a final warning announced that under no circumstances were gratuities to be given to the warders. Numerous members of the gentry who arrived exactly as instructed may, perhaps, have felt that they were a little more than April fools.

Some say that the custom goes back to Noah, who released his dove from the ark on the 1st of April when the earth was still covered by swirling waters; others that it is a world-wide relic of the ancient rites of spring.

14th April. Cuckoo Day.

The old lady used to take her basket and from it liberate the first cuckoo of the year at Heathfield Fair. That was in Sussex. In Worcestershire it was never heard before the 20th, when Tenbury Fair was held.

19th April. St. Alphege. Archbishop and Martyr.

This saint was brought up in the monastery at Deerhurst in Gloucestershire, and became abbott of Bath Abbey. His rule there ended the 'little junketings' of the monks. Later he was Archbishop of Canterbury when the Danes sacked and burned the place. They carried him off a prisoner to Greenwich. The devil appeared to him in his cell and tempted him to escape. He resisted and was martyred on this day in 1012.

21st April. St. Anselm. Archbishop.

Anselm was made Archbishop of Canterbury by William Rufus in 1093. A great theologian, he was successful as archbishop under three kings, and 'wrought admirable miracles.'

23rd April. St. George. Martyr.

George, says one story, was a high-ranking Roman officer until Diocletian issued a decree forbidding the practice of Christianity. This the saint not only refused to obey, but clad in full armour strode into the temple of Bacchus

E

at Nicodemia and smashed the official god. His resultant martyrdom took place on this day in 303.

Or if you prefer another version, he was an army contractor and 'big-business' man. A famous bacon contract scandal, his avarice and love of power made him thoroughly disliked. He was perhaps justifiably murdered by a mob. But in the course of his nefarious activities an archbishopric had come his way. This enabled his supporters to claim his death as martyrdom.

There are those who would say that it is typical of this country to chose as its patron a foreigner who has never even visited us. But the St. George that we know, the warrior-saint and slayer of dragons, is a very real symbol and has often been in our midst. He appeared to our Norman ancestors before Antioch in 1098; by 1222 he was so famed that his day was declared a holiday. At Agincourt he was seen in the sky above the English host. In the eighteenth century Pope Benedict XIV formally made him our protector.

His adventures with the dragon, which occurred at Silene, give the key to his character. The king's daughter, the prey of a dragon, was waiting her doom when George passed by. She besought him to help her to escape. But he refused, and replied that instead he would stay, defend her, and destroy the monster. When the terrifying beast arrived to seize its prey George armed with his great sword went in to the attack. After a fierce and noisy fight the dragon was so badly hurt that he was able to secure it, using the damsel's girdle as a lead. The procession moved towards the town, but instead of a triumphal entry it entered a place deserted. Seeing the dragon from afar the people had fled. However, they soon realized what had happened and returned marvelling. George then cut off the dragon's head, and taking advantage of the admirable impression that he had created, converted and then baptized all the citizens in the Christian faith.

The story, we are assured, is very similar to that of the heroes of other peoples. It is really the same as the legends of Perseus, Beowulf, and Siegfried. There are even parochial forms of it, such as the killing of the 'worm' by a member of the Lambton family.

Nevertheless St. George has become associated with innumerable guilds, associations, and traditions. The fine symbolism of his name has remained undimmed except during Puritan times.

The most famous order of chivalry was founded on this day in 1348.

Research has shown that the old accounts of its origin given by Polydore Vergil and Selden—for long disbelieved, perhaps because they were picturesque—are probably true.

At a celebration held by Edward III on the eve of his conquest of France, his loved Joan, Countess of Kent and Salisbury, dropped a garter to her embarrassment. The king picked it up and bound it round his own knee. There followed the usual suggestive remarks and titterings, which the king rebuked with the famous words 'Hony soit qui mal y pense,' adding that the garter would soon be greatly honoured. Before long he and his twelve knights of St. George—a league that he had formed to further his war—wore the blue ribbon; the following St. George's Day was the first Garter Day.

In medieval times St. George was a great popular hero, who had his part in the old mummers' plays, and in pageants and processions.

The cross of St. George is the English emblem in the Union Jack; the red rose of England is little worn on his day as unfortunately it flowers too late.

24th April. The Eve of St. Mark.

Any one having the courage to do so may await in a church throughout the night and see the spirits of those who are to die within the next year. The watcher must keep awake or else he too will join the spirits. The vigil, once kept, must be repeated yearly or death follows.

There are other ways of using this night to obtain a glimpse into the future. In the nineteenth century there still lived the custom of making a 'dumb-cake.' Three maidens mixed and baked it in silence. Then each broke off a third and at midnight retired to bed silently and walking backwards. Portents and visions then followed, which gave an insight into their matrimonial prospects.

Rather more simple was the practice of placing of nuts on the hearth. Each girl put down her own with the words:

> If you love me, pop and fly;
> If not, lie there silently.

25th April. St. Mark. Evangelist.

St. Mark, whose symbol is the lion, is traditionally the author of the second gospel. Little is known about him. He is reputed to have preached the gospel and presided over the church at Alexandria. Folk-lore and superstition are attached to the vigil rather than the day of his feast.

THE NATURALIST

The momentum of March has gathered strength, and even in our temperate climate growth and change proceed at an almost alarming rate; we are certainly bewildered by the innumerable changes so quickly passing by. The bird-watcher must have first place; May flowers come after April showers and cuckoos!

It is above all the month of migration. During its course most of our summer visitors arrive. Our remaining winter visitors leave, the migrant waders and the last fieldfare, redwing, wigeon, and jack-snipe.

A number of our natives and the earliest of our migrants are busy nesting, and those sea-birds which breed in colonies—such as gannets and terns—are no longer scattered over the seas, but congregated on the rocky islands and cliffs where they nest.

Arrivals are best listed. Here is the order displayed in a midland museum. The dates vary from place to place, and readers can argue about them—indeed about the order itself—to their hearts' content. Spaced from the 1st to the 31st, with a preponderance after the middle of the month, the catalogue runs: redstart, tree pipit, swallow, common sandpiper, house martin, cuckoo, nightingale, whinchat, grasshopper-warbler, sedge-warbler, lesser whitethroat, swift, common whitethroat, turtle-dove, wood-warbler, garden-warbler, and reed-warbler.

Two of these birds are among the stock properties of English literature—the cuckoo with his twin notes that 'change in June' (when they allegedly become triplicate) and the nightingale. The cuckoo, it is true, does make good use of its theme song, but almost equally heard are the bubbling, laughing, and chattering noises; the triple *cuck-cuck-coo* is also quite common during courtship. Male cuckoos are said to arrive first and predominate throughout the season. Nightingales sing just as much by day as by night. The song is rather difficult to pick out from the early morning chorus, but a little later in the day birds become quieter, and it is usually fairly easy to distinguish. The nightingale is a relative of the robin, as are the two species of redstart—the rarer black having come to live in our blitzed cities, to join another immigrant, fireweed.

It is in April that excited letters appear in the press announcing the rare sight of that remarkable crested, exotic looking bird, the hoopoe. It is, alas, only a bird of passage. We read that it has an engaging habit of throwing its food into the air and catching it before swallowing.

Roding, the courtship display of woodcock, is seen and heard in woodlands at evening. The bird makes regular, rather low circuits 'beating' or 'riding' the woodland glades.

All our native song-birds are singing during the month, as well as most of the arrivals. Practically all the residents are nesting. Early immigrants, such as the wheatear, have also begun.

It is always difficult to believe in the migration of butterflies and moths—far too fragile, it seems, to survive crossing the sea. But accounts of great clouds of them, sometimes literally taken for clouds, having been seen far from land, have been appearing for several centuries. The subject has been much studied recently, and careful records kept. Regular April migrants include painted ladies, red admirals, silver-Y and humming-bird hawk moths. Holly blues, commas, and small coppers are among other butterflies that will be found. Quite a number of moths are flying now. Those larvae that live through the winter or hatch early in the year are feeding vigorously in April, and my manual assures me that during this month I shall be able to stock my breeding cages liberally.

The observer of vegetation sees most marked and most lovely changes in the woods, for so many trees break their buds as if they were about to bear gold, bronze, or even pink leaves. Most of the April-flowering trees combine the opening of leaf with flower bud, and few now flower on bare twigs. The flowers open with the leaves on Norway maple and sycamore. The maple comes first, and provides an early and prolific source of food for bees. The oak catkins also open—they are the pollen-bearers scattering dust on very insignificant flowers which will be acorns. Oaks flower as the earliest bronze-coloured leaves open. The ash also flowers now, but before any vestige of foliage is seen. Those dark tufts which are the flowers sometimes cover the tree so thickly that they may be mistaken for breaking leaf buds; but, contrary to the popular saying, ash never leafs before oak.

The last of the poplars to flower and leaf is the giant open-limbed Italian black, so often host to mistletoe. It is a hybrid of unknown origin, and is propagated by cuttings or larger 'sets,' as it only exists as a male tree. The long red catkins fall almost soon after they open, before the bronze foliage flushes.

Birches also flower towards the end of the month with the opening leaves. The long, dangling catkins are male, carrying pollen to fertilize the more rigid, spreading or upward-turned seed-bearing catkins.

But the most lovely tree in April woods is our own gean or wild cherry; poets and authors have written of it so often that nothing more need be said of it now.

And there is no doubt that under the trees is April's real sight: a carpet of primroses and violets, with perhaps the first hazy smoke of bluebells. But there is even more to be seen, such as the early purple orchis and the spotted hoods of arum (or if you prefer it, cuckoo-pint, or even lords-and-ladies). Or in some woods butcher's broom is in flower—looking at the 'leaves,' like spine-pointed spades on playing-cards, you will find a minute flower in the middle—for on this odd plant the 'leaves' are really stems, and even more surprising, it is related to the lily. The delicate wood-sorrel will also be flowering, particularly in beech woods where little else grows.

The grass begins to grow in meadows, and buttercups come into flower; in damp meadows towards the south the chequered snake's-head fritillary blooms—a rarity if growing wild, but often effectively naturalized. But the most lovely flower of April meadows is undoubtedly the cowslip—the counterpart of the shade-loving primrose.

Broom is probably the most noticeable flower on commons, unless out-gilded by furze. On downland in very few places the pasque or Easter flower blooms, one of our most jewel-like flowers, a shade of violet with golden centre. It is an anemone whose richness and intricacy make a striking contrast to the frail windflower.

The seaside must be noticed this month, for thrift and sea-campion will be making patches of pink and white on the cliffs. The latter, *Silene maritima*, is believed to have survived the Ice Age in the British Isles.

There is as yet not much to see on hills and less on mountains, though against the damp, stream-side banks of the lower hills, golden saxifrage (*Chrysosplenium*) attracts attention with its minute, yellow flowers.

In the garden all is industry and preparation. Daffodils in a host of varieties are at their best. The stout columns of crown imperial topped with a cluster of yellow fritillary bells—dropping spots of dew and, for all their grandeur, smelling abominably—resist the stormiest April day. Forsythia, too, in its yellows, both pale and brassy, has, in the century that has passed since it came from China, been widely planted and now brightens up many a dreary spot where once spotted aucubas reigned supreme. Visitors to Kew and other gardens will have noticed the remarkable and lovely show made by the early magnolias flowering on their bare branches.

It is in the orchard that there is the gayest show. Damsons are first to flower, next the early pears, plums, and then cherry—later than our native gean—and finally the earliest, pink-flushed apple-blossom.

Of other life snails are on the move again; dormice and hedgehogs wake up for good. Toads make their annual journey to the ponds where they will breed. Frogs have got a lap ahead of them, and there will already be

Pheasant's Eye Narcissus

tadpoles hatched out. Newts also travel to water where they too will breed, carrying out an elaborate ritual as they court and fertilize their eggs.

Innumerable other events happen in April, yet only a few have been mentioned. Even so, I have given little more than a catalogue; but perhaps that is the nature of April, a catalogue of reviving life read through at breathless speed.

THE SPORTSMAN

Tradition and aristocracy on the one hand and modernity and mass popularity on the other are both catered for in April. For the former there is the ancient and at one time royal, but now rather forgotten, sport of otter-hunting; for the second—T' Cup.

Otter hunting is the only English summer sport in which hounds are followed. Otter hounds, in their oldest form (of which there are now but few packs), are distinguished-looking animals with shaggy coats. Short-haired hounds are, however, also used. Roger Follo was King's Otter Hunter to Henry II in 1175, and it is this which enables the sport to claim a royal and ancient history. Formerly the season was from Shrove Tuesday to Midsummer Day.

Fox hunting ends at some undetermined date during the month. On Exmoor hunting young stags finishes in the first half of the month.

The final of the Football Association Cup, played towards the end of the month, is perhaps the most largely attended of all our sporting events, attracting a huge democratic crowd. The spectators range from royalty to the humblest urchin. The anniversary of the first Cup Final is recorded under the month of March.

The horse plays an important part in April sport. In the middle of the month the London polo season opens. It was in its heyday during Edwardian times, when the great Hurlingham Club (founded in 1873) was at its prime. Country polo started much later in the year, and did not end until autumn, whereas London polo ended with 'the season' in early July. This Persian game, first played in England by the 10th Hussars in 1869, is, alas, really too expensive and spacious a luxury for our modern times—streamlined into mechanical austerity.

There are two big flat races at the end of the month. They form the first pair of the five 'classics' in the racing calendar. Both are included in the Newmarket First Spring Meeting, which begins in April, and continues into the first days of May. They are run on the Wednesday and Friday of the same week. First comes the Two Thousand Guineas. Founded in 1809 this is for three-year colts and fillies, and is regarded as a guide to the Derby. On the Friday comes the One Thousand Guineas for three-year-old fillies, which, racegoers believe, foreshadows form in the Oaks. This has been run since 1814.

About this season of the year many hunt point-to-point races also entertain the countryman.

A good deal of golf is played in April, including our amateur championship. This was first played over the St. Andrews course in 1886, having been sponsored by the Royal Liverpool Golf Club. Finally its control became centred in the Royal and Ancient Club. It was first won by an American, Walter Travis, in 1904.

There is one anniversary. On the evening of 27th April 1789 died Eclipse. He was in his twenty-sixth year and was, perhaps, the most famous racehorse of all time. The Duke of Cumberland bred him, but died shortly after he was foaled. A meat salesman then bought him for seventy-five guineas, but he changed hands until he eventually became the property of Colonel O'Kelly, who made £25,000 out of him at stud. Over one hundred of his descendants have won the Derby.

ANNIVERSARIES, EPOCHS, AND RECORDS

5th April 1845. After a preliminary examination by the architect Barry, members of the Government, and eminent scientists, the fountains in Trafalgar Square ('this truly scientific embellishment of the metropolis') played for the first time.

7th April 1349. William of Ockham (a village in Surrey) died—at least according to old reference books, but nowadays we are not so sure of the date. Continental scholars have given him the name of Occam; their enthusiasm for him seems now to be returning to the land whence his medieval fame originated. 'The invincible doctor,' as he was called, 'freed logic and empirical science from the tyranny of metaphysics.' His device, known as Occam's razor—a mental weapon highly esteemed by modern logicians, his treatises against the claims of the pope's temporal jurisdictions, and his championship of the rule of poverty in monastic life, all increase his stature in the eyes of the twentieth century.

13th April 1742. Messiah by G. F. Handel, one of the greatest works in English musical history, was first performed at the New Music Hall, Fishamble Street, Dublin. The words were compiled from the Scriptures by a wealthy amateur, Charles Jennens. 'Words are wanting to express the exquisite delight it afforded to the admiring crowded audience. The sublime, the grand, and the tender, adapted to the most elevated, majestic, and

63

moving words, conspired to transport the ravished heart and ear.' The composer and principals gave their proceeds, about £400, to charity.

16th April 1818. We can assign this day to the first public appearance of the kaleidoscope, an ingenious invention which achieved sudden and overwhelming popularity. Its originator, the eminent scientist, Sir David Brewster, would have made a fortune from it had not his idea been pirated.

16th April 1850. Another oddity is recalled by the death in London on this day of Mme. Tussaud, 'artist and exhibitor of wax figures.' She learned her art in Paris at the time of the Revolution, and had modelled Robespierre, imitated the horrible features of Marat, and made a likeness of beautiful Charlotte Corday. After her exhibition was opened in Baker Street she was always to be seen silently sitting among, and scarcely discernible from, her wax figures.

17th April 1802. Dr. Erasmus Darwin died. Few men can have done so much indirectly to alter the habits and thought of humanity. A leading member of the Lunar Society, in which was cradled modern industry, a poet, a speculative scientist and prophet of the theory of evolution, a successful doctor, friend and adviser of many of the finest brains of the day, he was above all literally the progenitor of a race of scientists, naturalists, writers, and artists—of whom Charles Darwin was one—that has left an indelible mark on the history of society.

His last day was typical: a letter written about a collapsible table, another comparing his home with Petrarch's Vaucluse, with some notes on his poetry; an argument with one servant who had neglected his horses, and with another for churning butter on Sunday; an attack of illness, and an easy, painless death. He spent his life in or near Lichfield.

19th April 1824. George Gordon, Lord Byron, died at Missolonghi in Greece, where he was supporting a revolution. Since his birth on 22nd January 1788 he had played consistently the role of aristocratic and romantic poet. We will, therefore, include him as our representative of this species, not very common in England.

19th April 1881. Another oddity thrown up by history, Benjamin Disraeli, later first Earl of Beaconsfield, died. He was born in London on 21st December

1805. An extravagant figure, an extravagant novelist, most flamboyant and un-English of men, his brilliant political career incongruously made him the corner-stone of English Conservatism.

18th April 1882. Charles Darwin died at Down in Kent, when he had long lived the secluded life of an invalid. Grandson of Dr. Erasmus Darwin, his father was a Shrewsbury doctor. As a young man he started to follow this profession, then, disliking it, turned towards the Church, but in the end sailed as a naturalist in the *Beagle* to South America. She left on her voyage of research under Captain FitzRoy, on 27th December 1831. Darwin returned in 1836; his journal of the cruise placed him at once among the greatest naturalists. His consequent researches and writings on the origin of species and theory of evolution undoubtedly qualify him as our April epoch-maker.

23rd April 1616. William Shakespeare died. We like to think that he was also born on this, St. George's day, in 1564. The greatest poet in the English language, his outlook is naturally more that of man from the heart of England, rather than of the city where he worked. From quite early times, though at first intermittently, his day has been kept at the town of Stratford-on-Avon, where he was born and died. Naturally Londoners have always disliked having to leave their grime and travel to celebrate in the fresh air. Consequently when a Stratford brewer (of all people) named Flower, and his friends, decided that the time had come to celebrate Shakespeare in his own town in his own theatre, the opposition from London became frenzied. However, the foundation-stone of the first and rather peculiar Memorial Theatre was laid with full Masonic honours on this day by the Lord Lieutenant of Warwickshire in 1877. It was now become a national institution, and the celebration of Shakespeare's day an annual international occasion—in Shakespeare's town, *not* London.

23rd April 1850. William Wordsworth, poet laureate, died. He was born on 7th April 1770. Undoubtedly one of our greatest English poets, he sees the world through very different eyes from Shakespeare's. The teeming Elizabethan world was not for this careful, successful man; rather does he wander (an umbrella hung over his arm) among metaphysical shades dwelling among the damp hills of the north.

28th April 1772. There died a goat that had twice circumnavigated the globe with no less a person than Captain Cook in the *Endeavour*. The Lords of the Admiralty admitted her as an in-pensioner of Greenwich Hospital. She is surely our April record-breaker.

THE POET

April is the first of the three months most frequently celebrated by English poets   From the earliest times to the present she (for April, being fickle, is feminine) has been chosen as the image of awakening youth.

But now all is changed.   Every schoolboy knows that Mr. T. S. Eliot considers that she is, among other unpleasant things, the cruellest month to the dead land.   A poetess has retorted that if he thinks this is so then he might well use his pen as a bayonet on which to skewer the 'catsmeat of his defeat.'

Let us, however, quote from happier days when gold rather than chromium was the currency of poets.   We could start with Chaucer and the ancients, but it is really not much use.   To all but a handful of experts the language they use is more foreign than French, so we will skip on to Edmund Spenser and his famed celebration both of April and his 'fayre Elisa . . . blessed wight, the flowre of virgins.'   The scene has the confusion and colour of an old tapestry.

> See, where she sits upon the grassie greene,
>   (Oh seemely sight!)
> Yclad in Scarlot, like a mayden Queene,
>   And ermines white:
> Upon her head a Cremosin coronet,
> With Damaske roses and Daffadillies set:
>   Bay leaves betweene,
>   And primroses green,
> Embellish the sweete Violet.
>
>   .   .   .
>
> Bring hether the Pincke and purple Cullambine,
>   With Gelliflowres;
> Bring Coronations, and Sops in wine,
>   Worne of Paramoures:

> Strowe me the ground with Daffadowndillies,
> And Cowslips, and Kingcups, and loved Lillies:
>> The pretie Pawnce
>> And the Chevisaunce,
> Shall match with the fayre flowre Delice.

Next we will jump the centuries to Browning's over-famous lines. Of a thousand, or a million, Englishmen who can and do quote them on every really bitterly cold and sleety April day, only a few will be able to continue:

> . . . whoever wakes in England
> Sees, some morning, unaware,
> That the lowest boughs and the brushwood shea.
>> Round the elm-tree bole are in tiny leaf,
> While the chaffinch sings on the orchard bough . . .

A lovely and typically Victorian sadness is found in William Allingham's lines beginning:

> Within a budding grove
> In April's ear sang every bird his best,
> But not a song to pleasure my unrest
>> Or touch the tears unwept of bitter love;
> Some spake, methought, with pity, some as if in jest:
>> To every word
>> Of every bird
> I listen'd and replied as it behove . . .

> The chaffinch, thrush, and black-bird mocked and only the robin
>> soothed.

As January has its wassailing songs and February its Valentines, so April has its cuckoo poems. The two notes, so significant when first heard, but soon to become exasperating, have been celebrated from the earliest days—as in the lines by an unknown author:

> She bringeth us good tidings,
>> She telleth us no lies;
> She sucketh all sweet flowers
>> To keep her throttle clear,
> And every time she singeth
> Cuckoo—cuckoo—cuckoo!
>> The summer draweth near.

The Elizabethans are, of course, full of the bird. So are the sentimental Georgians with, for example, Gray's conceit that:

> The Attic warbler pours her throat
> Responsive to the cuckoo's note. . . .

and Michael Bruce:

> O could I fly, I 'd fly with thee:
> We 'd make, with social wing,
> Our annual visit o'er the globe,
> Companions of the spring.

Wordsworth inevitably puts the bird into a sonnet:

> When sunshine follows shower, the breast can thrill
> Like the first summons, Cuckoo! of thy bill
> With its twin notes inseparably paired.

The two most famed Victorian cuckoos belong to Tennyson and Matthew Arnold. They do not belong to April, but are gloomy echoes of spring singing in June.

Finally there is W. H. Davies's famous cuckoo singing with a rainbow.

Returning to the main theme, it would be wrong not to refer to, even if we cannot quote, some of the modern April poets. First, I think, we must rank Robert Bridges. Then there are Thomas Hardy and John Drinkwater. John Masefield's

> . . . April 's in the west wind, and daffodils . . .

is often quoted, while his *Daffodil Fields* has many scenes in April. Edmund Blunden has written a disquieting poem, *April Byeway*. There is Walter de la Mare's

> I love thy cloudy face. . . .

And, now out of fashion, Sir William Watson's

> April, April,
> Laugh thy girlish laughter,
> Then, the moment after,
> Weep thy girlish tears! . . .

Or the Rev. Charles Tennyson Turner's Constable-like landscape in *An April Day*:

The lark sung loud; the music at his heart
Had call'd him early; upward straight he went,
And bore in nature's quire the merriest part,
As to the lake's broad shore my steps I bent;
The waterflies with glancing motion drove
Their dimpling eddies in among the blooms
Shed by the flowering poplars from above;
While, overhead, the rooks, on sable plumes,
Floated and dipt about the gleaming haze
Of April crost anon by April glooms,
As in the fashion of her changeful days;
When, what the rain-cloud blots, the sun relumes
O' the instant, and the shifting landscape shows
Each change, and, like a tide, the distance comes and goes!

But most descriptive and almost loveliest of all is W. H. Davies's *April's Charm*:

When April scatters coins of primrose gold
Among the copper leaves in thickets old,
And singing skylarks from the meadows rise,
To twinkle like black stars in sunny skies;

Green Woodpecker

When I can hear the small woodpecker ring
Time on a tree for all the birds that sing;
And hear the pleasant cuckoo, loud and long—
The simple bird that thinks two notes a song;

Then I can hear the woodland brook, that could
Not drown a babe, with all his threatening mood;
Upon whose banks the violets make their home,
And let a few small strawberry blossoms come:

When I go forth on such a pleasant day,
One breath outdoors takes all my care away;
It goes like heavy smoke, when flames take hold
Of wood that's green and fill a grate with gold.

Briefly and perfectly Shakespeare sums up (I said April was changeable, and now we see it even as to sex):

When proud-pied April, dress'd in all his trim,
Hath put a spirit of youth in everything.

MAY   TAURUS

MAY with thirty-one days is the fifth month of the year. The origin of the name is doubtful. The Roman festival of Maia, most luminous of the Pleiades sisters, was held in May. Possibly the name goes back to some word evolved from the Sanskrit root *mah*, grow.

One writer assures us that the Anglo-Saxons called it by the odd name of Tri-Milchi, the month when growing herbage enabled the cows to be milked thrice daily.

A wedding in May is considered unlucky. This because during the month Rome celebrated the festivals of Bona Dea, most chaste and matronly of all goddesses, and Lemuria, a remembrance of the unhappy, restless, evil dead who harass living mortals.

In some parts of the country hawthorn or may blossom is never brought into the house for fear of evil consequences. Dr. Vaughan Cornish has traced this superstition as existing in those parts of the country which were overrun by the Belgic people in the century that passed between Julius Caesar's departure and the invasion under Claudius. These people held hawthorn to be holy and to cut it was sacrilege.

May was, and in some places still is, the month of fairs. The May Fair ground in Piccadilly is now but a name, but in many an old town progress has failed to prevent the arrival during the month of stalls and roundabouts at their traditional sites, often in the main streets.

May was also the month when the annual meetings of religious organizations and public charities — missions, orphanages, asylums, and so on — were held. 'May meetings' will be found so defined in old reference books.

In a very mild way the old custom of going a-maying lingers, but at week-ends instead of on the first of the month, when fine days take townspeople out into the edge of the country. On Sunday evenings the roads are full of motorists and cyclists, the trains and buses of hikers, all returning tired from their outings. Nearly all carry huge bunches of bluebells which are stuffed into bowls and vases on the tables of their smoky homes and central-heated offices as a reminder of fresher air and a brighter outlook.

THE WEATHER

The saying 'Cast ne'er a clout till May is out' is by some said to relate to the month, by others to the tree. Meteorologically we are safe in applying it to the month.

Buchan has his third cold spell from the 9th to the 14th. This coincides with the days dedicated on the Continent to the ice-saints, when the weather is often extremely cold. Only one of them is well known to us, St. Pancras. The others are St. Mamertius and St. Servatus. It is not an uncommon occurrence for these cold polar airs to sweep over our country during the two middle weeks of the month. On the 17th in 1935 the thermometer at Greenwich fell to 28·2° F., the lowest reached. In 1891, on Whit Monday, the 18th, there was a heavy fall of snow, and many places had the only known opportunity for tobogganing on this holiday. Geoffrey Taylor [1] records how he watched, on the 11th, a brilliant display of tulips and other flowers projecting through snow, around which butterflies flitted—the scene 'in the highest degree curious—like an iced birthday cake sprinkled with those microscopic many-coloured sweets that we used to call hundreds and thousands.'

Yet in 1922 we had a London temperature reading during May of 91° F. The average is about 50° F.

On 13th May 1907 Alexander Buchan, F.R.S., died in his seventy-ninth year. In 1927 his researches first received quite unreasonable and distorted prominence in the press, and to-day more people have heard of Buchan's spells, hot and cold, than of practically any other feature of meteorology. The

[1] *Insect Life in Britain.*

so-called discovery of his 'spells' was the result of many years of meteorological and statistical research. From this he deduced that there were clearly defined periods when on an average those days between x and y were likely to prove either much colder or hotter than was usual for that particular period of the year.

Apart from the sound warning about sensible clothing, there are several proverbs assuring us that bad weather in May is good for us and vice versa:

> A cold May and a windy
> Makes a fat barn and a findy;
>
> A hot May makes a fat churchyard.

Findy, we learn, means weighty or massive.

THE HEAVENS

The sun remains in Taurus for the first three weeks, and then rises into Gemini, the Heavenly Twins.

FEASTS, FAIRS, AND FESTIVALS

1st May.   St. Philip and St. James the Less, Apostles and Martyrs.

St. Asaph.   May Day

It is regrettable that the festivals of these three saints (though the last is not kept by the Church) have never achieved the fame and reputation of our pagan May Day, nor apparently has the Church ever tried to invest them with relics of the heathen rites.

St. Philip was the disciple with whom Christ discussed the feeding of the multitude. His emblem is, therefore, a basket of loaves. St. James is shown carrying a fuller's club. After being thrown from the roof of the temple he was martyred with that implement. St. Asaph belonged, we are told, to 'the fabulous period.' He is connected with the city and cathedral in North Wales, of which he is patron.

On the other hand, although May Day is not honoured as it was in the good old times, it is far from forgotten and remains as a relic displaying simple pagan joy at the imminence of summer's return. Under the old calendar it was celebrated nearly a fortnight later in the year than now, on the 13th— a fortnight when flowers and buds are opening at breakneck speed, so that the festival was more likely to coincide with the flowering of hawthorn or may-tree. Despite its name, this tree was by no means the only one used or connected with the day. Birch was quite as important. Even to-day we may see birch saplings placed by cottage doors to bring luck. Other flowers belonged to the festival; school children made (and perhaps still make) cowslip balls for the occasion.

The celebrations took three forms.

First there was 'going a-maying.' Young men and girls went out, sometimes as early as the eve of May Day, to greet the earliest dawn. Then they returned with flowers and branches woven into garlands which they employed to decorate their houses or pile around the maypole on the village green. Dancing and other festivities followed. Perhaps justifiably, the puritans insisted these night-and-dawn adventures led to 'goings-on,' and the custom died out.

Hawthorn

Next there was the ceremony of erecting and dancing round a maypole. A May king and a May queen usually presided over the proceedings. Originally the 'pole' was a sapling tree, but later a pole decorated in many different styles was used. The largest in the land was put up in the Strand after the Restoration to replace one pulled down by order of the Commonwealth. It was 134 feet high and was hauled into position by sailors. May kings disappeared long ago, but queens are still chosen in some schools and villages, and a few maypoles still arise.

Finally there were dances, pageants, processions, and plays, many being of a kind peculiar to one locality. For example, there was the chimney-sweeps' dance which survived in London until the eighteen-seventies. A small party of sweeps, gaily dressed, danced around a strange figure called Jack-in-the-Green. He was almost hidden inside a framework covered with greenery and flowers, all being surmounted by a flag. Each party included one gaudily dressed woman. A drum and fife made the music; as the dance proceeded halfpennies were collected from the spectators.

There were, too, the processions of milkmaids which, if we are to believe the Georgian painters, made quite an idyllic scene. In our own times we still see a few horses beribboned for the day, a last reminder of the gay parades of decorated tradesmen's horse-drawn vans and carts. But petrol has now almost washed these away.

It is still the practice to decorate churches in some villages on May Day. A church service is also linked with a custom that lingers in the south-west. Children carry May dolls, believed to be effigies of the Virgin Mary, and beg for pennies. An occasional hobby-horse parade remains, such as that at Padstow, when the 'animal' suffers a ritual death.

May Day is, above all, the day for greeting the magical dawn in the fields and woods, and by the singing of songs in high places. The choir still sings at dawn on Magdalen Tower as it has done for ages—perhaps even before the present tower was built. It is also welcomed by song at the church of Bargate near Southampton.

Above all, if you can bathe your face in dew collected at May dawn—or better still, kiss the dew as it lies on the grass at sunrise—it will bring you beauty.

3rd May. Invention of the Cross.

This oddly named festival celebrates the invention, or discovery, of the cross on which our Saviour was crucified. One legend has it that Empress Helena, mother of Emperor Constantine the Great, journeyed to Jerusalem to seek the cross. Many crosses were found. On each a dead man was placed until on one the corpse miraculously came to life. Then all the beholders knew that the true cross had been found.

Once found the cross was placed in a church specially built by the emperor in Jerusalem. Chosroes, King of the Persians, later stole it, but Emperor Heraclius recaptured and returned it to the proper place with great ceremony.

6th May.   St. John the Evangelist before the Latin Gate.

On this day the Church celebrates the occasion strangely referred to in the twopenny calendars as *ante P. Lat.* The story is that in his old age a rival sect accused John of atheism. Near the Porta Latina in Rome its members placed him in a cauldron of boiling oil. Miraculously he was in no way harmed by this unpleasant experience.

7th May.   St. John of Beverley.

On this day in 721 died John, Bishop of Hexham, and founder of the monastery of Beverley in Yorkshire. He had a remarkable effect on bulls; the fiercest of them when dragged into Beverley churchyard became as docile as lambs. The Church no longer remembers him.

8th May.   Furry Dance, Helston, Cornwall.

By some this festival is held to be a relic of the May feast held in Roman days to honour the goddess Flora—Furry being a corruption of *Floralia.* It starts with the old May custom of 'fetching the summer home'—houses being decorated with greenery early in the day, which is entirely devoted to festivity. There is a children's dance in the morning, and then the Invitation Dance at noon. For this men wear morning coats and buttonholes, and women their best summer frocks and lilies of the valley. As they dance the couples knock at every door; should one be open they go through the house, the men bowing and the women curtsying to any person met in the passage. This brings summer luck to the household. Unusually this ceremony has never been connected with the Church and has always remained purely secular.

19th May.   St. Dunstan.   Archbishop.

Born at Glastonbury this west-country saint died as Archbishop of Canterbury on this day in 988. He was a remarkable man, of whom are recorded numerous miracles, some against and others reputed to be for the devil. Of the former we are told that when working as a goldsmith (a craft at which he was skilled) the devil appeared. Dunstan picked up a pair of red-hot tongs, and with them seized the Satanic nose. He held on until late at night, the

77

devil roaring and crying all the time. In view of this harsh treatment the Devon story shows that both had a forgiving nature. It happened at the time St. Dunstan set up as a brewer of ale. The native cider was far too popular and the saint was not prospering. So he bartered his soul to his former enemy the devil, who as payment gave an undertaking that on the three mornings that ended with what is now Dunstan's feast there would be such frosts as would destroy the apple blossom and put an end to competition from cider.

25th May. St. Aldhelm. Bishop.

This saint died in 709. He founded the abbey at Malmesbury, and is said to have been the first Englishman to cultivate poesy. One day, while he was saying mass, his servant carelessly dropped his cloak. Aldhelm picked it up and hung it on a sunbeam.

26th May. St. Augustine of Canterbury. Archbishop.

The anniversary of the death in 607 of the monk who was sent to England by Pope Gregory I for the purpose of converting us to Christianity. This he accomplished, and became the first Archbishop of Canterbury. He was certainly helped by his power of working miracles, for in one village whose inhabitants behaved in a particularly reprehensible manner, and proved specially unconvertible, he arranged that all the children should be born with tails until the people repented of their evil ways.

27th May. The Venerable Bede.

The Church remembers the death of this great scholar—'the father of English history'—in 735. His learning made his school at Jarrow in Northumberland the literary centre of western Europe.

His eloquence was such that when, aged and blind, he was led by a deceitful man to preach to a pile of stones, the effect on them was so great that at the end of the discourse they one and all answered 'Amen.'

29th May. Oak Apple Day.

On this day, his birthday, in 1660, Charles II entered London for the first time since the execution of Charles I, and so re-established royalty. This was celebrated by the common people (who had suffered from the petty restrictions of Puritanism) wearing oak leaves or oak apples. This recalled the story of Charles hiding in an oak-tree at Boscobel in Shropshire during his flight. The house of the Penderel family, who succoured him on this occasion, still exists. The oak was long ago replaced by one of its seedlings.

To-day the Grinling Gibbons statue of Charles II is garlanded with oak branches. It stands in the grounds of Chelsea Hospital, whose Founder's Day this is. The pensioners eat plum pudding into which a sprig of oak is stuck instead of holly.

At Wishford in Wiltshire the villagers have a right to gather dry wood from the forest of Grovely, and on this day to cut the heaviest oak boughs that they can carry without mechanical or animal aid (bicycles and handcarts, but no other vehicles, may be used). The men rise early and march to the woods in procession, with a banner bearing the words 'Grovely! Grovely! and all Grovely! Unity is strength!' The boughs are gathered, brought back, and leaned against the houses. A further ceremonial procession follows, and the day ends with feasting and sports.

The day is also celebrated at the Leycester Hospital at Warwick, at Worcester Guildhall (outside which is an odd statue of Charles), at Northampton (for which town Charles provided timber after its great fire of 1675), and by a procession of the Garland King and Queen at Castleton in Derbyshire.

THE SPORTSMAN

It is our native green turf that makes the month for sportsmen, both of the energetic and more peaceful types. May brings it into the prime of condition —firm, springy, and, unlike all other surfaces, alive.

So we have cricket. And lawn tennis, croquet, bowls—but, above all, cricket, most English of games, full of our defects as well as qualities.

Few sports have been more written about, for it is a game loved by authors. No doubt it was derided by some and worshipped by many when played on the village greens in some form or another during the seventeenth century; by 1750 it was sufficiently organized for the formation of the famous club at Hambledon. The game became more serious and approached its modern form with the coming into being of the Marylebone Cricket Club in 1788. One of the first recorded matches played on its ground was on 16th May 1791 —for one thousand guineas, let us note!

On 2nd May 1814 T. Lord respectfully informed the Noblemen and Gentlemen, Members of the Marylebone and St. John's Wood Cricket Clubs, 'that his new ground was completely ready, and that the first meeting would be held on 9th May.'

The Marylebone Cricket Club from its headquarters at the present Lord's ground still dictates how the game shall be played.

Our great rivals, Australia, first visited us in 1878. On 27th May of that year they defeated a powerful M.C.C. side in one day.

But an even quieter and much older game, bowls, draws more players to the green than does cricket to the pitch. It seems to be a highly civilized form of the primeval and fascinating diversion of rolling stones. At one period it was so popular with youths that it endangered the practice of archery. To-day most of the players who from May onwards tread goloshed and gingerly on the nurtured turf are a little concerned with their girth, as well as with the course taken by their rolling woods—a course inexorable and undeterred by cries, moans, coaxing, and the most magnetic gestures.

Lawn tennis begins now, and also has early origins. It is generally held to be a much simplified outdoor form of tennis—possibly the oldest organized ball game in existence. In its present form it is quite a modern game, having developed during the eighteen-seventies. In 1877 the All England Club at Wimbledon remodelled the laws and equipment, and from that date its popularity has increased greatly and spread all over the world. Like bowls, it is played on surfaces other than grass, but in England the summer tennis-lawn remains supreme.

Croquet is said to derive from the thirteenth-century *paille-maille*. Its establishment in this country was due to a Miss Macnaughten, who brought it via Ireland from the south of France. She organized games on the lawns of Lord Lonsdale's garden in 1852. The first public match was played at Evesham in 1867. A year later the first all-comers meeting was held at Moreton-in-the-Marsh, and the All England Croquet Club was formed. This skilful and malicious game has declined in popularity; it retains some of its glory at Cheltenham and other places where old memories linger on.

In the latter half of May Eights week takes place at Oxford; the college rowing eights attempt to 'bump' the boat ahead of them. It is also something of a social occasion for youth, beauty, and parents of members of the university.

THE NATURALIST

May flowers have been promised first place. We shall start with trees. The almanacker has, throughout the months, given them a good deal of prominence. Comparatively few in number, as beautiful when bare as covered with leaf, growing both in towns and country, all we need is an upward glance when walking past to see that the phases of the year are there displayed for us to mark.

In May, then, there is a continuous show of the real flowery kinds: from pears and cherries at the beginning of the month to horse-chestnut, lilacs, and laburnum at its end. The last three may give the exile nostalgic thoughts of spring in English gardens—of London parks in particular. But they are really foreigners that we have adopted. Laburnum and lilac came from southern Europe in the sixteenth century. Except for a little lengthening of its golden chains, laburnum has remained unchanged since its arrival. But nurserymen, particularly in France, have done wonders with lilac, varying the size and colour of its flowers—though all remain lilac-scented. It is also amenable to the skill of florists, and townsmen looking into their shops might well think that it flowered naturally in January. Horse-chestnut looks a bit of a foreigner. In winter it bears delightful sticky buds on twigs springing from branches which bend in curves unlike the shape of any other English tree. It was first grown here in the early seventeenth century. For a long time botanists thought that it came from India, but its real home, where it is quite uncommon, is in the Balkans. Sticky buds are followed by candelabras of flowers borne against the rich-coloured and woolly textured young leaves. Finally it gives us mahogany 'conkers'—which surely were designed purposely to entertain children.

Our native whitebeam and rowan also flower. The first of these rosaceous trees vies with the gean as being the loveliest we possess. None of our trees, except the white willow, has more silvery leaves.

Undoubtedly one of our three most famous May sights is the carpet of bluebells in woodlands. Few bulbs, fortunately, are more persistent. Vast numbers are ruthlessly pulled up each spring, but the survivors still carpet the woods.

Hollies flower. The male trees bear pollen which covers the visiting bees and insects with grey powder. Female trees, which alone in autumn carry the red berries, have nectar-bearing flowers. Very rarely a tree has flowers of both sexes.

Against the ever-increasing green of the woods—some trees, such as the limes and horse-chestnut, are now quite umbrageous—those cautious few—ash, robinia, black Italian poplar, mulberry in orchards and catalpa in London parks—stand naked and black for long. But by the end of the month they too are coming into leaf—mulberry and robinia flower as they break, but the 'Indian bean' or catalpa (which comes from the United States of America) waits until late summer.

Once again we are in danger of compiling a catalogue, which will not only be tedious, but almost endless, so let us take a more erratic course.

First to strange orchids. Some are at their best in May. The green-winged and purple, man, monkey, spider and fly, the rare military—all are exciting enough as names alone to encourage us in a fascinating hunt for native kinds. One of our rare plants of the lily family, the four-leaved herb Paris, is equally a source of magic and surprise, and is now found flowering.

These are plants that lure us with their mystery. But who bothers to look at the May-flowering meadow grasses, such as the sweet-scented vernal, fox-tails, and cat's-tails? Their flowers and pollinating mechanism form an equally absorbing, if at first sight less glamorous, subject for study. But as the old custom of hay-making is gradually replaced by cutting for silage, grass flowers may become sufficiently rare to attract us!

The meadow brings us two other sights which are, I think, most typical of May. There is first the pale golden blossoming of innumerable buttercups, and then by its side, wherever there is a ditch or wide grassy verge, an even border of white filigree—cow-parsley or wild chervil.

These three—bluebells in the woods, buttercups in lush meadows, and cow-parsley by the wayside—give us the essential qualities of May.

In the garden we have oriental cherries and a plethora of shrubs. Particularly do we now see rhododendrons and azaleas from almost all over the northern hemisphere in their blazing and lovely colours. In this century the flora of China, much of which is May-flowering, has quite altered the aspect of our gardens. It also is the month when the rockery (called by some, alpine garden) is at its best. Tulips are out and the first iris. We will not dwell on the other May garden flowers; they are better known than most, for the first warm sunshine brings everybody from houses into gardens, as well as from towns into the countryside. We will, therefore, run the risk of omitting the reader's own favourite and pass on to the ornithologist.

Practically all birds are now nesting or rearing their young. All are singing, too. The misselthrush alone begins to tire. Stability of the bird population is more or less reached; migration has for a moment practically ceased.

The few late-comers are either delightful or distinguished. There

Nightjar

is the swift or jack-squealer, to whizz in parties with a whistling scream around tree tops and houses—or to wheel, a minute speck, at a great height. This indicates (as they say) that the weather will be fine. The weather-lore experts can seldom have noticed how high they go on some thundery, stormy days. The spotted flycatcher returns. This is another bird we can watch with ease and pleasure as he sallies from his perch, to which he quickly returns having caught his fly. We hear, too, the soothing murmur of the little turtle-dove—a sound of summer days. Then there is the nightjar, who spends the day crouching along a branch, and in the evening makes his gentle 'churr'—an unbird-like sound, a rather mechanical noise like some small and delicate machine that runs without a break for a minute or so and then suddenly stops. Also at night may be heard the passing whimbrel, known as the may-bird, or from its cry, the titteral and seven-whistler.

The only gloom to be found in May bird-life is among the ducks. At the end of the month many drakes go into eclipse, losing all their finery and appearing much like their wives.

All our animals are active again. Many are breeding. Young squirrels, stoats, weasels, shrews, moles, and in wilder places, polecats are to be found. Fallow deer drop their horns.

As for the insects, 'May, like Pandora, opens her casket of winged creatures —midges and gnats, and coarse-bodied flies as annoying to mankind as the evil sprites in the legend, and butterflies, rainbow-hued and beautiful as that other last imprisoned spirit—Hope.'[1]

Taking them in that order we can start with the may-bug or cockchafer, that lumbering, buzzing beetle, who flies in the evenings. Its loathsome-looking grub may spend as long as five years living on the roots of trees. When at last it is transformed the beetle carries on with the damage by eating their leaves and shoots.

The first of the damsel or demoiselle flies leave their ugly earlier skins behind, and emerge as flying jewels. Later in the month the short-bodied dragon-fly *Libellula* is out. The demoiselles are frail and wandering in flight, *Libellula* darting and determined.

Of butterflies and moths, so many kinds are now flying that we again risk catalogue-making. Let us simply choose names that sound nice, rare though some of the creatures be: swallow-tail (in the fens), black-veined white (now extinct, but once a dweller on Muswell Hill), Bath white, orange tip; pearl-bordered, greasy, and Glanville fritillaries (*Euphrosyne*, *Aurinia*, and *Cinxia*); the green hair-streak and small copper; common, holly, and mazarine blues; of moths, the wood tiger and small lappet, the alder kitten and puss; the mullein, betony and starwort sharks; the lunar double stripe, scalloped hazel, and brindled beauty; white wave, netted mountain, the ruddy and May highfliers and the pugs, the flame carpet and small phoenix.

If butterflies and moths teach us a May lesson, it is that they have been named by poets—which is only right and proper, for May is the poet's month.

[1] Vere Temple, *Butterflies and Moths in Britain*.

ANNIVERSARIES, EPOCHS, AND RECORDS

1st May 1851. The Great Exhibition of the Industries of All Nations was opened by Prince Albert. Held in Hyde Park it was housed under a gigantic glass roof held by an iron framework covering 1,000,000 square feet. Later this Crystal Palace was transported to Sydenham. The exhibition continued for 141 days. Both because of the original design of the buildings, conceived by Sir Joseph Paxton, and as the first of the modern monster shows, this event deserves to rank as our May epoch-maker.

7th May 1663. The original Theatre Royal in Drury Lane was opened with a performance of *The Humorous Lieutenant* by Beaumont and Fletcher. Pepys complained of the acoustics; he could not hear 'the basses of the musique at all, nor very well the trebles.'

14th May 1842. The *Illustrated London News* was first published. For sixpence a week it gave you thirty engravings. The forerunner of a host of competitors, it still happily holds its own.

14th May 1941. The first aeroplane to have a jet engine was successfully flown. This device, which converts the energy of burning fuel into motive power without any intervening complication of pistons and cranks, was engineered by Sir Frank Whittle. The flight was made at Cranwell, Lincolnshire. A sister engine had, however, become unofficially airborne at an earlier stage.

26th May 1703. Samuel Pepys died. The son of a London tailor, he was born on 23rd February 1632. We can commemorate him either as the author of an unashamed diary of a typical unimaginative, worldly, but rather sentimental middle-class Londoner, or, as he became later in life, Secretary of the Admiralty, a wise and courageous administrator, and an exemplar to the civil service of later days. But perhaps most of us prefer the knowledgeable fellow who was husband to the beautiful, clever, and temperamental Elizabeth St. Michel, and wept at the sound of beautiful music.

28th May 1741. Thomas Topham, the Strong Man of Islington, lifted unaided three hogsheads of water. These were roped to a yoke carried over his shoulders.   The feat was performed before a crowd at Bath Street, Cold-bath Fields, in commemoration of the capture by Admiral Vernon of Porto-bello.   As the weight lifted was some 1,800 lb. we are justified in hailing the feat as our May record.

30th May 1842.   Police-constable Tounce, A 53, was patrolling Constitution Hill at a quarter past six in the evening when he seized John Francis, who was just firing a shot at Queen Victoria.   As a result the bullet went harmlessly into the air.

THE POET

April is the month of youth, then May is the month of love ('Love, whose month is ever May'), of flowers and the nightingale.

First, to choose a few of the lovers.   There are Nicholas Breton's Phillida and Coridon at cross purposes in the sixteenth century:

> In the merry month of May,
> In a morn, by break of day,
> Forth I walk'd by the woodside,
> When as May was in his pride.
> There I spiéd all alone
> Phillida and Coridon.
> Much ado there was, God wot!
> He would love and she would not.

Tragic was the famous occasion when:

> All in the merry month of May,
> When green buds they were swellin',
> Young Jemmy Grove on his death-bed lay
> For love of Barbara Allen.

Or we can become rather more complex in our emotions and quote Coventry Patmore:

> 'Twas when the spousal time of May
> Hangs all the hedge with bridal wreaths,
> And air 's so sweet the bosom gay
> Gives thanks for every breath it breathes,

When like to like is gladly moved,
  And each thing joins in Spring's refrain,
'Let those love now, who never loved;
  Let those who have loved love again';
That I, in whom the sweet time wrought,
  Lay stretch'd within a lonely glade.

Then there is the peaceful scene described by Hartley Coleridge in *May 1840* with its evocation of lovers:

A lovely morn, so still, so very still,
  It hardly seems a growing day of Spring,
  Though all the odorous buds are blossoming,
And the small matin birds were glad and shrill
Some hours ago; but now the woodland rill
  Murmurs along, the only vocal thing,
  Save when the wee wren flits with stealthy wing,
And cons by fits and bits her evening trill.
Lovers might sit on such a morn as this
  An hour together, looking at the sky,
Nor dare to break the silence with a kiss,
  Long listening for the signal of a sigh;
And the sweet Nun, diffused in voiceless prayer,
Feels her own soul through all the brooding air.

And the warm-blooded call of Herrick to his Corinna to rise and go a-Maying:

See how Aurora throws her fair
Fresh-quilted colours through the air:
Get up, sweet slug-a-bed, and see
The dew bespangling herb and tree!

Next, on turning to the flowery May, we have majestic Milton unbending:

Now the bright morning-star, Day's harbinger,
Comes dancing from the east, and leads with her
The flowery May, who from her green lap throws
The yellow cowslip and the pale primrose. . . .

A lord high chancellor of England in the last years of the eighteenth century, Lord Thurlow, is best remembered by his poem *May*:

May! queen of blossoms,
And fulfilling flowers,

With what pretty music
Shall we charm the hours?
Wilt thou have pipe and reed,
Blown in the open mead?
Or to the lute give heed
In the green bowers?

Thou hast no need of us,
Of pipe and wire;
Thus hast the golden bee
Ripen'd with fire;
And many thousand more
Songsters, that thee adore,
Filling earth's grassy floor
With new desire.

Thus hast thy mighty herds,
Tame and free-livers;
Doubt not, thy music too
In the deep rivers;
And the whole plumy flight
Warbling the day and night—
Up at the gates of light,
See, the lark quivers!

Now we must consider Philomel, who replaces the cuckoo in the time of

Fast fading violets cover'd up in leaves;
And mid-May's eldest child,
The coming musk-rose, full of dewy wine,
The murmurous haunt of flies on summer eves. . . .

Having so remembered Keats we may turn back to the Elizabethan Richard Barnefield:

As it fell upon a day
In this merry month of May,
Sitting in a pleasant shade
Which a grove of myrtles made,
Beasts did leap and birds did sing,
Trees did grow and plants did spring;
Everything did banish moan
Save the Nightingale alone:

She, poor bird, as all forlorn
Lean'd her breast up-till a thorn,
And there sung the dolefull'st ditty,
That to hear it was great pity.
Fie, fie, fie! now would she cry;
Tereu, Tereu! by and by;
That to hear her so complain
Scarce I could from tears refrain;
For her griefs so lively shown
Made me think upon mine own.
Ah! thought I, thou mourn'st in vain,
None takes pity on thy pain:
Senseless trees they cannot hear thee,
Ruthless beasts they will not cheer thee:
King Pandion he is dead,
All thy friends are lapp'd in lead;
All thy fellow birds do sing
Careless of thy sorrowing:
Even so, poor bird, like thee,
None alive will pity me.

So I might go on quoting, for I find that I have accumulated more for
May than any other month.   The moderns have been neglected.   But how
can I find room for them when there is still the speech from *The Knight of the
Burning Pestle* spoken by a May-lord, standing 'upon a conduit, with all his
scarfs about him, and his feathers, and his rings, and his knacks':

Rejoice, O English hearts, rejoice! rejoice, O lovers dear!
Rejoice, O city, town, and country! rejoice, eke every shire!
For now the fragrant flowers do spring and sprout in seemly sort,
The little birds do sit and sing, the lambs do make fine sport;
And now the birchen-tree doth bud, that makes the schoolboy cry;
The morris rings, while hobby-horse doth foot it feateously;
The lords and ladies now abroad, for their disport and play,
Do kiss sometimes upon the grass, and sometimes in the hay;
Now butter with a leaf of sage is good to purge the blood;
Fly Venus and phlebotomy, for they are neither good;
Now little fish on tender stone begin to cast their bellies,
And sluggish snails, that erst were mewed,[1] do creep out of their shellies;

[1] Shut up.

The rumbling rivers now do warm, for little boys to paddle;
The sturdy steed now goes to grass, and up they hang his saddle;
The heavy hart, the bellowing buck, the rascal,[1] and the pricket,[2]
Are now among the yeoman's peas, and leave the fearful thicket:
And be like them, O you, I say, of this same noble town,
And lift aloft your velvet heads, and slipping off your gown,
With bells on legs, and napkins clean unto your shoulders tied,
With scarfs and garters as you please, and 'Hey for our town!' cried,
March out, and show your willing minds, by twenty and by twenty,
To Hogsdon or to Newington, where ale and cakes are plenty;
And let it ne'er be said for shame, that we the youths of London
Lay thrumming of our caps at home, and left our custom undone.
Up, then, I say, both young and old, both man and maid a-maying,
With drums, and guns that bounce aloud, and merry tabor playing!
Which to prolong, God save our king, and send his country peace,
And root out treason from the land! and so, my friends, I cease.

[1] A lean deer.   [2] A buck in his second year.

JUNE  GEMINI

The sixth and midsummer month. The number of days was not finally decided until Julius Caesar fixed it as thirty.

The origin of the name is obscure. The goddess Juno, the *juniores* of Roman legislature, and the consulate of Junius Brutus are to be found among the explanations.

Anglo-Saxons called it the 'dry month.'

It is the time of haysel. Over most of the country the hay crop is made and carried. *Haysel* has already disappeared from some dictionaries. The old, seemingly eternal sight of hay-making itself may follow it into oblivion as more and more grass is cut while it is still short and turned into silage.

June is a garden month, the florist's triumph. He sees the results of his work on roses, irises, sweet peas, and many other favourites. They have left nature far behind, and though they do not often surpass her in grace or fragrance, they exceed her in gaiety and size; indeed, man's flowers are often stupendous, and even fantastic.

It is now not enough to long for the waterside, where the herbage grows long and lush. We envy the fisherman, as yet surrounded only by the flies loved of fish and not by the horde of buzzing, biting, and stinging insects that pursue him later in the season.

THE WEATHER

Science justifies the phrase 'flaming June'—if indeed averages prove any-thing. For records establish June as, on the average, the sunniest and possibly driest, but not the warmest, month of the year. On the other hand,

some of our most famous rainstorms, sometimes associated with thunder of mythological force, have happened in the month. The wettest day on record was at Bruton in Somerset on 29th June 1917. Over nine and a half inches fell in twenty-four hours.

Ground frosts are not uncommon, and sometimes air frosts. Very rarely snow falls. The normal temperature is about 56° F.

Buchan's fourth cold spell starts on the 29th and lasts into July.

THE HEAVENS

In June the sun achieves his greatest mastery. On the 21st or 22nd (more frequently on the 21st), as he passes from Gemini to Cancer, the Crab, occurs the summer solstice, the day when he shines for longer than on any other— some sixteen hours and thirty-nine minutes in London. He rises and sets in the north-east and north-west. Once the solstice is passed the nights again become longer.

FEASTS, FAIRS, AND FESTIVALS

5th June. St. Boniface. Bishop and Martyr.

This English saint, born at Crediton, and educated at Exeter, achieved fame and success on the Continent, where he became primate of Germany and Holland. We are told that he was particularly skilful at converting the pagan, but that his miracles were, alas, no more than pious frauds.

11th June. St. Barnabas. Apostle and Martyr. Barnaby's Day.

'And Joses, who by the apostles was surnamed Barnabas (which is, being interpreted, the son of consolation), a Levite and of the country of Cyprus, having land, sold it, and brought the money, and laid it at the apostles' feet.' Beyond that we know little of this saint. He spent the rest of his life propagating the gospel; it is said that he founded the bishopric of Milan, and was martyred in Cyprus. As our own Barnaby he presides over the hay harvest, carrying a rake.

In the ancient days there was a walnut-tree at Glastonbury that did not open its buds until this feast, after which it grew like any other. In slightly less ancient days it died, and was replaced by another of a perfectly ordinary kind. Yet this obtained a reputation of having remarkable if invisible qualities. King James I was one of those who had a scion from it.

17th June. St. Alban. Martyr.

Alban was born at Verulam in Hertfordshire, and went to Rome, where he became a soldier. On returning to England he embraced Christianity and tried to convert his fellow countrymen. He was, however, slain at the orders of Diocletian (the date is said to be 304), and became the first English martyr. Miracles were wrought at his martyrdom.

Some five hundred years later Offa, King of the Mercians, built a fine monastery near Verulam, which was the beginning of the town of St. Albans.

23rd June. Midsummer Eve.

The great bonfires for the fire festival of St. John the Baptist were built on this day ready to be lit on the stroke of midnight.

It is also a night of magic. Young men achieved invisibility if they could collect the minute seed from ferns. There was one condition: they must gather it on a plate without ever touching the fern itself.

Maidens could divine much about their future. They could, for example, take shoots of orpine (*Sedum Telephium*), and put them in their rooms. If the leaves bent to the right a lover was true; if to the left false. Hence the name still used for this plant 'midsummer men.' The hypericums or St. John's worts were, of course, most powerful at this season and much used for decoration.

24th June. Nativity of St. John the Baptist. Midsummer Day.

In pagan days the summer solstice was greeted with huge bonfires and fire rites of atavistic origin. The Church was able to move the celebration of these primitive customs a day or two forward, and attach them to the feast honouring the birth of St. John the Baptist. Several reasons were found which made the transition quite easy. For instance, the Emperor Julian so strongly agreed with the decision of Herod that he ordered the bones of the Baptist to be burnt by fire.

So the great fires, kindled at midnight as the day entered, blazed furiously in honour of a saint instead of a sun. As dawn broke men jumped girls through the embers or drove cattle through the ashes to bring luck and protection against disease—relics of the sombre times when living sacrifices were made to the flames. It was also a great day for fireworks, but these, like the bonfires, disappeared with nearly all midsummer celebrations during the last century, and now only appear at the one remaining fire festival, which has become attached to the memory of poor old Guy Fawkes.

One ceremony does, however, remain, although it fell into disuse for a long time. Lady Knollys put up a bow window in Seething Lane without having first obtained permission of the City of London authorities. She was punished by having to pay a fine of 'one red rose fresh pluck'd from the garden.' This was first paid in 1346. The custom lapsed, but now once again the lord mayor receives his rose. The home of Lady Knollys became the site of All-Hallows-by-the-Tower, whose churchwardens now pay the quit-rent that they inherited.

The puritans naturally stopped most of the celebrations on this day, particularly dancing and pageantry. One procession at least was revived with the restoration of Charles II. We have a description of its progress through Chester. In its ranks were the devil, the child Jesus, the four giants, the flower-de-luce, a camel and a dragon with boys to belabour them, a unicorn, and the elephant and castle in which sat Cupid armed with a bow.

26th June.

A famous fair was held within the precincts of the great abbey in the little town of Pershore. (The cuckoo was never heard in Worcestershire after it was over.) But in 1830 the genteel element won a long-drawn battle and the fair was thrown out of the abbey grounds into the streets.

29th June. *St. Peter the Apostle.*

In his later days, it is said, Simon Peter the fisherman founded the Roman Church, which gained its eventual world-wide authority through him. This generous impulsive creature, of whom we read in the Scriptures, eventually became the fine old man of stained-glass windows, patron saint of fishermen, and holder of the great keys to the door of heaven.

We may refer on this day to the old ceremony of rush-bearing. The aisles of churches were, of course, strewn with rushes as a floor covering. Their annual replacement was a great religious occasion. It is supposed to have been done on the patronal day of the church, but because St. John and St. Peter were greatly favoured as patrons, and because the job would have to be done in summer, it seems appropriate to mention it now.

The rushes were loaded on a wagon which was gaily decked with branches and garlands. It moved to the church in a grand procession, sometimes led by dancers. The rushes were then ceremoniously laid, usually in symbolic patterns.

Sometimes grass is still brought in place of rushes. It may be strewn over graves as well as aisles.

THE SPORTSMAN

In June the turf is still soft and green and is, or should be, shone upon by a genial midsummer sun. So our sporting events are now also social events; beauty adorned (even in June, a little hazardously) joins with grim and serious man in taking his relaxation. Once upon a time June was the height of London's 'season'—its events were patronized by society as well as attended by the crowds. We had the Derby and Royal Ascot; later Wimbledon joined them as a fashionable event.

But before we discuss these great occasions we must mention that one overriding passion of the common—and, in fact, nearly every—man, can now be lawfully assuaged: the coarse fishing season in fresh water opens on 16th June.

And now back to possibly our greatest national institution, the Derby. Until governments decreed otherwise this was run on the Wednesday of the week that included 31st May. In other words, Derby Day was generally the first Wednesday in June at Epsom. The story of its origin is that at a dinner party given by Lord Derby in 1779 at his house, Lambert's Oaks, at Woodmansterne, he and Sir Charles Bunbury laid down the rules for two races. One was to be for three-year-old fillies, the other for three-year-old colts and fillies. The race for fillies only was run on 14th May 1799 and won by Lord Derby's own Bridget. This race was named the Oaks Stakes after the house where the race had been arranged. Next year, 1780, the race for colts and fillies was run for the first time, and was won by Sir Charles Bunbury's

Diomed (one of the greatest horses of all time), and became known as the Derby.

Within a short time Derby week at Epsom became a great festival of racing. The Derby itself on Wednesday, and on the Friday after, the Oaks, are respectively the third and fourth of the five 'classics' run under Jockey Club rules. The extension of the railway to Epsom brought even greater crowds. In 1840 Queen Victoria and Prince Albert paid the Derby its first royal visit.

In the middle of the month comes Ascot week. 'Royal Ascot' has long been famed as an 'occasion of the highest social importance, combined with a high level of racing throughout the programme.' The meeting, held on the edge of Windsor Park, was established in 1727 by the Duke of Cumberland, uncle of George III. Everything about it is regal. The races include the Gold Cup, run since 1807; the Royal Hunt Cup, founded in 1843 and traditionally watched by royalty; and once upon a time the Emperor's Plate given by the Tsar of Russia.

The championships of the All-England Lawn Tennis Club take place at Wimbledon. It has long attracted an international entry, and many thousands of spectators. The tournament is a long-drawn-out affair, and finals week may extend into July, but to all but the very successful entrants it must rank as a June event.

At Cambridge the May Races are held. Now somewhat inaptly named, the races are the counterpart of Eights week at Oxford. Like that occasion it was included as a society event when, in Edwardian days, calendars of such things were published.

Those then are the sporting high lights of flaming June. But do not forget that in 1867 the future Lord Chaplin won the Derby when it was run in a snowstorm.

THE NATURALIST

As the summer solstice draws near we should recall those events in natural history which remind us of a flaming sunny month—though in our fickle climate we often enough have cold and gloomy June days. Which kind of naturalist shall receive first place? To the botanist, because to him is assigned the vegetable strawberry, 'the very primrose of fruits,' and the early cherries, both of which assure us that 'the rigours of spring are over'? To the ornithologist? Or to the entomologist? I was decided in my choice by a June news-cutting in my collection which recorded how that most exotic of our rare visitors, the golden oriole, had reached Lancashire. I am aware that normally it visits us earlier in the year, but the poetic juxtaposition of gold and grey, of the Mediterranean and Bolton, made me give the birds first place. So we will begin by recalling that it is in June that another excitement, the red-necked phalarope, arrives in British waters to breed.

Butcher Bird (and Larder)

One other arrival, though he may have been in the south during May, is the butcher bird or red-backed shrike. He is famous for the habit of catching his food—large insects and sometimes the smallest animals and young birds—and impaling it on thorn-spines or even barbed wire. Thus he provisions a larder.

Otherwise migration has ceased. Nearly all kinds of birds are now nesting, or more probably raising their young, a number of which, including the game birds, are seen about.

Many kinds of drake are now in eclipse. Missel-thrush and great tit have ceased singing; the nightingales and other song birds are getting past their best and at the end of the month become quiet.

It is difficult to give adequate treatment to the botanist; in June full many a flower is born to be omitted by the almanacker.

At the beginning we have two big shrubs found at the edge of woodland in flower—our own guelder rose and the foreign rhododendron. The first carries its white flowers in globular clusters, small ones in the centre, which do all the work and produce those lovely translucent red berries in autumn, and big, showy, white blossoms at the edge which are sterile. A form which has even bigger clusters composed only of sterile flowers is grown in gardens and known as the snowball-tree; its owners miss the berries. The 'wild' rhododendron is that known as *ponticum* in botanical language, which describes it as coming from the shores of the Black Sea. Though it will only grow in an acid, sandy, or peaty soil, in many such places it has become very much at home, and grows into gigantic clumps. It was introduced, it is said, no earlier than 1763. In forests the pines, our own Scots and Austrian and Corsican, are flowering—the small catkin-like clusters of male flowers shed clouds of pollen when disturbed by the wind.

At the end of the month elder opens its broad white corymbs of bloom. It is one of those plants that love waste places. By old ruinous buildings, where left neglected and undisturbed (they say that where elder is allowed to grow freely there is always peace), it reaches the size of a tree. Thousands of bushes in flower make a remarkable sight on the spoil-banks of the industrial midlands and north, where it is an ardent colonizer. Sometimes to be found, as often as not growing with elder and flowering among ruins, are the poisonous and sombre henbane, thorn-apple, and deadly nightshade—*Hyoscyamus*, *Datura*, and *Atropa*, all containing the drugs atropine and hyoscine. They were once cultivated for their medicinal, and perhaps lethal, qualities. *Datura* came originally from Peru, but has now spread over much of Europe, the United States, and Russia. These plants of the shadows come only to relieve the galaxy of June flowers which are primarily sun-lovers.

Again we must avoid a catalogue, and we may do so by asking a question: What then are the June flowers? My answer is this: in the woods, creeping jenny or yellow pimpernel and the early honeysuckle; in copses, clearings, and on shady hillsides, foxglove; by streams, yellow flag iris, and meadow-sweet; in hedgerows, the wild roses.

Then we must have a word about the flora of bogs and damp, peaty places, which with our mountain flora is now beginning to reach its best. We will recall as typical *Drosera*, the sticky-tentacled sundew catching flies; succulent and damp-looking *Pinguicula* or butter-wort with pale yellow flowers; the delicate little yellow spikes of bog asphodel; pink, creeping bog pimpernel; in more marshy places that beautiful member of the gentian family, buckbean, with trifoliate leaves—but again, we are merely reviving our catalogue.

In the garden we have all those things that we associate with gay, coloured pictures in nurserymen's catalogues. The list includes plants of unbelievable loveliness—roses, peonies, bearded iris, sweet peas, delphiniums—all those flowers for which our gardens are famed.

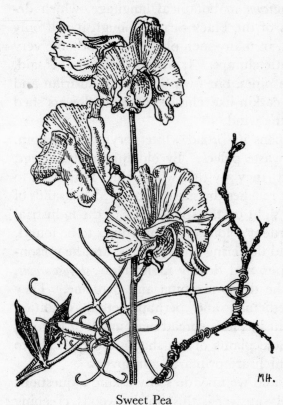

Sweet Pea

The entomologist, coleopterist, and lepidopterist have a glorious time. Flies, bees, wasps of all kind abound. There are still more dragon-flies. Flies of the waterside are abroad— the angler's may-flies and stone-flies, known to experts as *Ephemeroptera* and *Plecoptera*. In the south giant stag-beetles take to the air. On commons the grasshoppers chirrup.

In butterflies and moths there is a great increase. A selection from the poetical appendix to my manual to be added to the May list is as follows: ringlet, large heath, black hair-streak, large blue, large skipper, Duke of Burgundy, and the skippers. Of moths there are so many more that we will merely note that in June there is a considerable increase in the number of quick-flying hawk-moths. Larvae of all kinds are abundant—as the gardener notices.

The young of most of our mammals are now about—young badgers may be seen, given patience and luck. Voles are born. Young hedgehogs will also be seen in the evenings. The young of red and fallow deer are born; the former lie helpless for a week or so, the latter can run almost at once. Prickets, the second-year males of fallow deer, drop their horns.

As June ends the energy that comes from the sun has passed its zenith, but its momentum is now stored in the earth and we move forward to July by imperceptible stages.

ANNIVERSARIES OF EVENTS, EPOCHS, AND RECORDS

2nd June 597. Ethelbert, King of Kent, was baptized by the monk (later Saint) Augustine, who had been sent by Pope Gregory I to convert the English to Christianity. It is said that the ceremony took place at Canterbury and was the first official recognition of the Christian faith in England.

3rd June 1657. William Harvey, M.D., died. He was born of Kentish yeoman stock at Folkestone on 1st April 1578. A distinguished physician, he made the great discovery of the circulation of blood under the action of the heart. Though this subject formed part of his lectures from 1616 onwards he published no account of it until years after. He laboured successfully for improvements in the standards of medicine and surgery.

7th June 1832. It was Henry Crabb Robinson who wrote in his diary: 'This day will form an epoch in the history of England. The Royal Assent was given to the Reform Bill!' That epoch-maker opens our June epoch.

12th June 1842. The Rev. Thomas Arnold, D.D., was 'suddenly removed from his earthly duties and anticipated enjoyments by an attack of angina pectoris' in his fifty-second year. At thirty-one, though without experience as a schoolmaster, he was induced to offer himself for the vacant headmastership of Rugby school. One of his testimonials read 'If Mr. Arnold were elected he would change the face of education all through the public schools of England.' This came quite true after his appointment in 1828. Holding the post for nearly fourteen years he then became professor of modern history at Oxford.

18th June 1815. On a Sunday the Duke of Wellington, in command of a small army, held the French forces until the Prussians arrived. There followed a victory which ended once and for all the attempts of Napoleon to dominate the world.

The duke was granted an estate at Strathfieldsaye. His heirs still pay for this with a tricolour flag handed over on the anniversary of the battle and then hung on the Iron Duke's bust in the guard-room at Windsor Castle.

1835. William Cobbett died; he was born at Farnham, Surrey, of peasant stock, on 9th March 1762. We select him for commemoration as an English type. He made his way as soldier, journalist, publicist, and agricultural expert. In America he was a jingo Englishman; in England he was generally 'agin the government.' A professed reformer, he was opposed to progress, and considered that the cultivation of the potato would ruin agriculture. He was, however, undoubtedly successful in two things—arousing opposition, and writing superlatively good descriptions of the English countryside through which he rode.

20th June 1819. The *Savannah* (Captain Rogers) steamed into Liverpool, the first steamship to cross the Atlantic. She had taken 29 days 11 hours over the voyage from Savannah; off Ireland she was nearly stuck through lack of coke, but her sails pulled her through.

23rd June 1775. In spite of bad weather the first English regatta took place on the Thames. Lady Mary Montagu had returned from Italy with a description of a water fête that she had seen—it was called a *regatta.* London had as good a river as Italy, so why shouldn't we have one too? So the idea was given effect, most suitably on Midsummer Eve—but long after Lady Mary had died.

27th June 1787. On this night at Lausanne Edward Gibbon finished writing *The History of the Decline and Fall of the Roman Empire.* He walked under the acacias: 'The air was temperate, the sky was serene . . . I had taken an everlasting leave of an old agreeable companion, and reflected that whatever might be the future fate of my History, the life of the historian must be short and precarious.' Fate decreed fame for the History; the author died, aged fifty-seven, in 1794.

On the same day in 1723 a letter signed 'Anonymous' in the *Weekly Journal* described a most disgusting sight seen in Hyde Park—one of His Majesty's officers drinking tea. The writer suggested that *real* girls should officer the army if the practice continued.

THE POET

It was in late June that the steam hissed, a throat was cleared, and for a minute a blackbird sang, as a train, bearing the poet Edward Thomas, pulled up by the bare platform at Aldestrop.

In June, too, Mr. W. H. Auden (or a friend) lay out at night. His toes seem to have developed shapes like those depicted by Mr. Stanley Spencer in his less realistic pictures, but in spite of this he gazed happily at the night sky until interrupted by loud noises-off in Poland.

But above all June rhymes both with moon and tune, and is therefore the supreme month for the ballad-monger as well as for greater poets.

In Coleridge's time the month had been recalled by the ancient mariner:

> . . . yet still the sails made on
> A pleasant noise till noon,
> A noise like of a hidden brook
> In the leafy month of June
> That to the sleeping woods all night
> Singeth a quiet tune.

June days are also part of the month's poetic stock-in-trade. They are seldom so delicately used as in James Russell Lowell's lines:

> And what is so rare as a day in June?
> Then, if ever, come perfect days;
> Then Heaven tries earth if it be in tune,
> And over it softly her warm ear lays.

June nights are also famous:

> In a bowl to sea went wise men three,
> On a brilliant night in June. . . .

More conventionally we have them described by James Thomson:

> O, how the nights are short,
> These heavenly nights of June!
> The long hot day amort
> With toil, the time to court
> So stinted in its boon!

But three or four brief hours
  Between the afterglow
And dawnlight; while the flowers
Are dreaming in their bowers,
  And birds their songs forgo;

And in the noon of night,
  As in the noon of day,
Flowers close on their delight,
Birds nestle from their flight,
  Deep stillness holdeth sway:

Only the nightingales
  Yet sing to moon and stars,
Although their full song fails;
The corncrake never quails,
  But through the silence jars.

So few brief of hours of peace;
  And only one of us. . . .

Then we have the June cuckoo:

He was but as the cuckoo is in June
Heard, not regarded.

which was far from being so in those lovely lines by Matthew Arnold:

So, some tempestuous morn in early June,
  When the year's primal burst of bloom is o'er,
  Before the roses and the longest day—
When garden-walks and all the grassy floor
  With blossoms red and white of fallen May
  And chestnut-flowers are strewn—
So have I heard the cuckoo's parting cry,
  From the wet field, through the vext garden-trees
  Come with the volleying rain and tossing breeze:
The bloom is gone, and with the bloom go I.

Possibly the least conventional June poem is Leigh Hunt's *To the Grass-hopper and the Cricket:*

Green little vaulter in the sunny grass,
Catching your heart up at the feel of June,
Sole voice that 's heard amidst the lazy noon,
When even the bees lag at the summoning brass,
And you, warm little housekeeper, who class
With those who think the candles come too soon,
Loving the fire, and with your tricksome tune
Nick the glad silent moments as they pass:
Oh sweet and tiny cousins, that belong,
One to the fields, the other to the hearth,
Both have your sunshine; both, though small, are strong
At your clear hearts; and both seem given to earth
To ring in thoughtful ears this natural song—
In doors and out, summer and winter, Mirth.

But I think we must regard June as the month of blue skies and long sunny days, sparkling stars and full moons if short nights, of roses and bird-song and ballads (even though it doesn't often happen quite like this). So we cannot end more suitably than with W. E. Henley's *Ballade of June.*

Lilacs glow, and jasmines climb,
  Larks are loud the livelong day.
O the golden summer-prime!
  June takes up the sceptre of May,
  And the land beneath her sway
Glows, a dream of flowerful closes,
  And the very wind 's at play
With Sir Love among the roses.

Lights and shadows in the lime
  Meet in exquisite disarray.
Hark! the rich recurrent rhyme
  Of the blackbird's roundelay!
  Where he carols, frank and gay,
Fancy no more glooms or proses;
  Joyously she flits away
With Sir Love among the roses.

O the cool sea's slumbrous chime!
  O the links that beach the bay,
Tricked with meadow-sweet and thyme,
  Where the brown bees murmur and stray!

Lush the hedgerows, ripe the hay!
Many a maiden, binding posies,
Finds herself at Yea-and-Nay
With Sir Love among the roses.

Envoi

Boys and girls, be wise, I pray!
Do as dear Queen June proposes,
For she bids you troop and stay
With Sir Love among the roses.

JULY   CANCER

JULY is now the seventh month, with thirty-one days.   It is named in honour
of Julius Caesar, who, in addition to his achievements well known to those
who learn Latin, is famous in the history of almanackery.   In 45 B.C. he
exercised a privilege enjoyed only by the very powerful—the introduction of
a new calendar.   It was worked out for him by an Egyptian astronomer
named Sosigenes, but Caesar naturally took the credit for putting it into
effect, and it was called the Julian calendar.   This system was generally used
until further improvements were ordained by Pope Gregory in 1582.   The
Gregorian calendar is still current.

Before Caesar's time the old name for July, Quinctilis, the fifth month, had
clung on from the period before January and February were included in the
calendar.

The Anglo-Saxons gave July several names.   One was Mædmonath—
the month when the meadows flowered.

In England it seems, apart from one famous attempt to invade us, to have
been the most peaceful and uneventful month of the year.   During the dog-
days few birds sing.   True high summer is reached and we may pause and
survey the scene.   All the gay spring colours have gone.   Woods and fields
are in their deepest and richest greens.   We see the England of our classic
painters, a landscape still and calm, under massive, umbrageous trees.
Hedgerows are full of the larger flowers, hills and moorlands beginning to
glow with colour.

But in the city the air becomes dull and parched as the smoky fumes stifle
the effort that the trees and little grass plots make each year to be bright and

green.   They become drab and dingy once again in their failure, and instead the rosebay creeping about makes a pink glow in the waste places.

The tiredness of towns affects its inhabitants as the month goes on; it is no new symptom of the citizen, for the Victorian Robert Chambers described it in his *Book of Days*: 'We feel the harness in which we have so willingly worked amid "the fuss and fret" of the busy city, and pine to get away to some place where we can hear the murmur of the sea, or what is nearest the sound—the rustle of the summer leaves.'   So he longed, as we all do, for the seaside or the country where 'it is now July and the world's great eye, the sun, is mounted on the highest loft of the horizon.   The grasse of the mountains withers, and the parched earth would be glad of a draught of raine to slake her thirst.   Nor doth the farmer make ready his teame, and the carter with his whip hath no small pride in his whistle.   The cannons of heaven begin to rattle, and when the fire is put to the charge it breaketh out among the clouds, and the stones of congealed water cut off the eares of the corne. The cuckoe spits and storms, and the blackness of the clouds affright the faint-hearted.   The stag and the buck are now in their pride and their prime, and the hardness of their heads make them fit for the horner. . . .   The rivers are now more wholesome and delightful than the baths.   Be sure every morning to perfume your house well with tarr and engelica seeds burnt in a fire-pan or chafing dish of coales than which nothing is better. . . .   The recreations and country contentments properly appertaining to this month are, bathing and swimming in the cool and christall rivers.'

Matthew Stevenson.   1661.

THE WEATHER

Every Englishman believes in his heart of hearts that this is dependent on St. Swithin's Day—should that be wet, then we can be sure of rain on the next forty days.   Yet every year our betters prove to us statistically that this is the most fallacious of legends.   In fact July is normally the warmest and one of the driest months of the year in all parts of the country, except perhaps those near our western and southern sea coasts.   In recent times St. Swithin's legend has only been right once—in 1930—and then not over all the country.

The Roman belief that the heat of the 'dog-days' (3rd July to 11th August) was because the dog-star, Sirius, rose and set with the sun, was rather more in accord with events if not with this cause. For statistics and Buchan in particular show that the 12th to the 15th inclusive are likely to be extremely hot; they form the first of Buchan's so-called hot spells, and on one of them, the 15th in 1881, our hottest day occurred. The temperature rose to just over 100° F. at Alton in Hampshire.

In these islands the first days of July are, however, usually cool, and Buchan's fourth cold spell ends on the 4th.

The average temperature for the month is upwards of 60°—the figure we are all taught to believe is perfect.

THE HEAVENS

About the 21st the sun passes from Cancer into the sign of Leo, the Lion.

At the end of the month it becomes quite apparent, however much we try to ignore it, that the evenings are drawing in. The sun sets half an hour earlier at the end than in the beginning of the month. There is a still greater difference in the times of sunrise, but it still occurs at an hour when few of us are about to be depressed by it.

FEASTS, FAIRS, AND FESTIVALS

3rd July. St. Phocas.

Next to nothing is known of this saint, and his life, miracles, or martyrdom, except that he was a gardener at Sinope in Pontus. He is therefore the patron saint of gardeners, and as such must be mentioned in our English almanac. He is also highly thought of by Greek sailors.

5th July. Midsummer Eve, Old Style.

It is said that in Northumberland bonfires are still made and danced round on this night.

12th July.   Vintners' Procession.   Swan Upping.

The Master, Wardens, and Members of the Worshipful Company of Vintners go in procession to a service at the church of St. James, Garlickhithe.   They are preceded by two wine porters sweeping the street with besoms.   Then follow the beadle, the stavesmen, the swan-marker, and the barge-man.   The officers carry bunches of scented flowers, which, with the sweeping of the besoms, are reminders of the filthy state of the streets at the time of Edward III in whose reign the company received its charter.

Mute Swan

Later in the month its Swan Master meets the Keeper of the Royal Swans and the Swan Master of the Dyer's Company.   They proceed in six beflagged boats from Southwark Bridge for the annual swan upping, wearing their striped jerseys.

The two companies have shared with the king the ownership of swans on the Thames since the Middle Ages, when the swan was a royal bird and valuable.   The birds are now examined and marked to show ownership.   The young are marked on the beaks with one nick if belonging to the Dyers, two for the Vintners; the king's swans remain unmarked.

The marking takes several days and ends with a banquet.   Roast cygnet is served.

15th July.   St. Swithin.

He was Bishop of Winchester from 852 to 862, and later for a few centuries its patron saint.   During his lifetime he is reputed to have been an architect and builder of churches.   After his death his body was placed, in accordance with his humble nature and at his request, outside the church in 'a vile and unworthy place,' where the sweet rain of heaven might fall upon the grave. His present meteorological fame dates from the year 971 when, on 15th July, following his adoption as the patron of Winchester, the officials attempted to remove his remains to a better situation in a new basilica more fitting to a saint. The gentle spirit of Swithin objected, however, and arranged for a deluge which lasted forty days.

Other countries possess saints whose spirits have behaved in the same way. But they fail to time their downpour to coincide with the fall brought about by our St. Swithin.

25th July. St. James the Apostle.

The anniversary of his martyrdom. His body is said to have arrived miraculously in Spain, of which country he later became patron saint. Probably that is why we hear much of him in English legend, though he is well known to us as patron of famous churches, a great palace. and a park.

One little custom may remain. Children set up grottoes made from oyster shells, and beg pennies with the words 'Please to remember the grotto.' This is because when the saint's headless body was making its miraculous journey to Compostella in Spain, borne in a marble ship, it floated over a horse and rider which were drowning. They were saved by the power of James; as the man rode out of the water his cloak was seen to be covered with scallop shells. Hence shells have remained an emblem of the saint; according to some, oysters come into season on old St. James's Day—on which, incidentally, Thomas Hickathrift killed the giant near Lynn.

THE SPORTSMAN

Except possibly for the finals at Wimbledon and an occasional test match there are no great excitements in the sports world, no great events draw men in thousands from their work, no red-letter day in the calendar marking a battle whose outcome the nation awaits breathless and expectant.

Probably the nearest approach to it is our Open Golf Championship, but the man in the street is probably only concerned to the extent of having half-hearted hopes that a Britisher will win. It was first played at Prestwick in

1860, and for some years continued at that club. It is now in the hands of the Royal and Ancient.

The Oxford and Cambridge cricket match really sets the gentlemanly, leisurely pace for the month.

The most popular and widely followed sport during July is that of the humble angler with his worm or grub, patiently waiting for perch, roach, or other of the coarse fish, whose season is now at its height. The banks of ponds, rivers, and canals are lined with these static fishermen, who have been brought from the towns by train, bus, charabanc, and cycle. Each sets up a little encampment, and spreads his paraphernalia, prominently including bottles of beer.

The more genteel and mobile forms of fishing, with flies after quarry of a better social standing, also proceed with vigour.

In the evenings suburbia tries to emulate the stars of Wimbledon, and in quiet old places the click of the balls in croquet, now the poverty-stricken but genteel sister of lawn tennis, may still be heard.

It is the month for other sporting events in which quality rather than quantity counts. They were among the last engagements in the old London season when Society still existed.

There is the annual regatta for amateur oarsmen at Henley-on-Thames, which has been held, with rather fluctuating fortunes, since 1839. The principal events, with their glitteringly named trophies, are world renowned: the Grand Challenge Cup for eight-oar crews, the Silver Goblet for pair oars, the Diamond Sculls for single sculls, and the Ladies' Challenge Plate for crews from schools and colleges.

Then two race meetings—one very distinguished—are held. In the middle of July there is Sandown, famed for the Eclipse Stakes, which was founded in 1884 as the first race to be run for a prize of £10,000. At the end of the month are held Goodwood races. This meeting was established in 1802 by the Duke of Richmond, and is held on the edge of his wooded park in the downland of west Sussex, within sight of the Channel. His predecessors first went there (in 1720) to hunt, and it was not until the Earl of Egremont ceased holding races at Petworth that the Richmonds replaced them by those on their own ground. From the first it has, as an old writer says, 'always attracted horses of high character.'

THE NATURALIST

As if to balance the richness and variety of vegetation birds become quiet and sing no more. The woods become silent as, perhaps, life becomes easier for them and, ragged and dull, they go into partial retirement. Old cuckoos leave our shores for the south—though the cuckoo's departure is much less publicized than his arrival. We all know, however, that 'In July away he fly,' or, according to fancy, buries himself in the mud of ponds, or, as some say, turns into a hawk.

The cuckoo's departure is but one sign that bird movement is under way again; the waders are among the first to be on the move. Most birds having finished nesting are dispersing around the countryside, and many kinds may be watched in quick succession as they pass along hedgerow or through woodland. July is the month when crossbill invasions occur.

The larger and stronger plants, those able to fight their way through the lush growth of grasses, now flower in the hedgerows. Meadow-sweet and valerian are to be found in the damp places, and round them hovers the demoiselle—the 'blue thread loosen'd from the sky.' Elsewhere along the roadside the coarser umbellifers abound, handsome structures mounted with their umbrellas of dingy-white flowers which, as often as not, are covered with colonies of little beetles and strange flies. Honeysuckle is in the woods, and our more magical herbs are represented by the St. John's worts and enchanter's nightshade, for which Linnaeus, displaying his usual perfect taste in apt selection, chose the lovely name of *Circaea lutetiana*, which, from botanical Latin, may, I suppose, be translated into 'The Enchantress from Paris.'

The blue forget-me-nots are everywhere. The old name of scorpion-grass may hint at the similarity of the uncurling flower stem to a scorpion's tail, but how innocent of sting or anything other than purity it is when uncurled and opened ready, we imagine, to give the fatal stab!

That is one of the smaller flowers now open. Others are to be seen on the heaths and hills. The pink glow of the heathers, the delicate harebell, and, where there is limestone, the yellow rock-rose opens in the sunshine for an hour or two before the petals tumble away.

> In the breeze
> That wafts the plumed thistle's seed along
> Bluebells [1] wave tremulous.   The mountain thyme
> Purples the hassock of the heaving mole,
> And the short turf is gay with tormentils,
> And bird's-foot trefoil, and the lesser tribes
> Of hawkweeds; spangling it with fringed stars.

Around the edges of pools water plantain, arrow-head, and rushes form, with their clear-cut geometric designs, a margin to the dark mirrors on which float water-lilies—the white one so beautiful that it is dedicated to the nymphs, and the yellow ending its days as a comic brandy bottle.   In damp spots there are pink patches of bog pimpernel, and, in some places, the exciting sundew is hard at work catching flies while its flower stems uncurl.

Indeed, the end of July is the time when the marsh flowers come to their best; the unblossom-like flowers of the bulrush *Typha latifolia* are seen, and also those of yellow monkey-flower or mimulus—an American that has become naturalized in many damp places, and is related to the musk that so mysteriously lost its scent.

It is the month of the great exodus of little frogs, no longer admitting that they were once tadpoles, from their ponds.   They are often so thick upon the ground that it is impossible to avoid walking on them, and millions must perish when their march to dry land happens at the same time as the mowing of grass.

Two famous weeds, obnoxious, but not without beauty, become ubiquitously prominent towards the end of the month.   Both seem to be hand-in-glove with man and his doings, delighting particularly in the waste places that he makes.   The first of these to gain a reputation was the ragwort, *Senecio Jacobaea*.   With brassy daisy-flowers and fancifully cut, even tattered leaves, it can be seen in every dry desolation, along roadsides, and particularly in poverty-stricken meadows.   In any quantity it is poisonous to stock, as is its relative, groundsel, if given in too large doses to canaries.   Both belong to the same family as the candlelike succulents of African mountains.   Ragwort is a menace to farmers and an increasing nuisance everywhere.

The other pest is the graceful rose-bay willowherb, the townsman's fireweed.   This lovely plant, with its tall spikes of slender leaves ending in a

[1] In the north bluebell is the happily chosen name of our harebell; it can surely ring more freely than our southern stiffly sprung bluebell!

spire of rose-pink flowers, thrives equally well in ground that man has cleared or left derelict, either in town or country. In autumn the long thin pod splits, and the two parts curl back and scatter innumerable seeds, each with a tuft of down, which float gently in clouds and spread all around. The young plant roots but lightly in the surface, and as soon as it is established sends out runners, each of which will send up another spike. It quickly spreads, forming a mat of choking vegetation. Its increase during recent times has been surprising, and is now alarming. Probably the clear felling of woodlands during and after the 1914–18 war gave it a good start. It now colonizes clearings so quickly and effectively that it is swamping and perhaps destroying the smaller plants that would usually grow in such a place— probably altering the whole nature of the vegetation. It has spread to spoil-banks and ground that has been cleared of buildings, and seems especially happy in the wake of a fire, for its network of roots thrive in the arid, crumbly surface that is left. For these reasons it has spread more and more during the last decade, an aftermath of war that has delighted in the acres of wood-land that have been felled and the blocks of cities which bombs have razed and burnt. In flower it is a lovely sight, and loved by the honey-bee for the nectar it carries. The bee-keeper knows when his hives are working the waste lands, for his bees return dusty-white from the fireweed's pollen.

The citizen has two other flowers this month. Wherever privet has escaped the clippers it bursts into blossom with rather drab little spikes that look like, and are, very poor relatives of the white lilac. The scent is heavy, sickly, and symptomatic of high summer in suburbia. It is liked by the bees, but their keeper objects to the honey they make from it. The heavy flow of nectar produced by the lime on warm still days—sometimes so freely that it can be shaken from the flowers—is, however, a joy equally to the bee and his owner. In a good year many a town hive's crop is of its dark rich honey. The trees are often golden with the blossom, and the sweet scent of lime avenues, or even single trees, drifts along the city streets as a reminder of old lime walks in country churchyards and parks.

Another forest tree, the sweet or Spanish chestnut, is also in flower. It is often densely covered with white, spreading catkins, thick with pollen. At their bases hide the female flowers with their feeler-like stamens which catch the pollen, are fertilized, and soon develop into chestnuts.

The insect world has a great month.   The song of the grasshopper is heard again on sunny days, and at night the first glow-worms may be seen.   If the weather is right ants may swarm out of the nest, and the winged generation take to the air and mate.   Butterflies abound.

'Let us, therefore, seek the half shade of the woodlands, where are to be found in July a galaxy of beauties: White Admirals, fritillaries that rival them in grace, and Purple Hair-streaks, the females of which reflect the royal colour of that monarch among our butterflies, *Apatura iris*, the rare and splendid Purple Emperor. . . .   I have spent un-forgettable days in the July woods, watching the soarings and alight-ings of this beautiful butterfly.' [1]

White Jasmine

The first home-bred generations of what we might call our own domestic or garden butterflies hatch out—peacock, tortoiseshell, red admiral, and painted lady—sometimes while their immigrant parents are still on the wing; the humming-bird hawk-moth hovers in our gardens, and sometimes the newspapers get excited over invasions by the clouded yellow.

The gardener begins to harvest, as do the fruit-eating birds (perhaps that is why they are silent).   There are now the finest cherries, red, white, and black currants, raspberries, the last of the strawberries, and dessert gooseberries.

Vegetables abound, and though the season of the aristocrats of the flower garden is passing, the herbaceous borders are gay with the achievements of nurserymen; the sweet-scented white jasmine of the poets is covered with flowers.

And we must not forget the lesser plants, for in July 'the deep rocky lanes abound with *filices* and the pastures and moist woods with *fungi*.'

[1] Vere Temple, *Butterflies and Moths in Britain.*

ANNIVERSARIES OF EVENTS, EPOCHS, AND RECORDS

1st July 1536. Henry VIII forced the Right Reverend Father in God, William Boston, and the Convent of Westminster, to hand over to him the Manor of Hyde. His reforming zeal was directed to the preservation of hare, partridge, pheasant, and heron, but under later sovereigns the manor developed into our famous Hyde Park. It later became the preserve of orators as well as herons, and by a coincidence on the same day in 1855 the first big political demonstration was held there. A crowd estimated at 150,000 was broken up by the police.

4th July 1862. 'All in the golden afternoon' and during an expedition up the river to Godstow, the young Liddell sisters bewitched the Rev. C. L. Dodgson so that he became Lewis Carroll, who started telling them about the adventures of Alice.

4th July 1776. In America Congress formally adopted a resolution concluding with the words: 'We, the representatives of the United States of America . . . appealing to the Supreme Judge of the world for the rectitude of our intentions, solemnly publish and declare that these United Colonies are, and of right ought to be, Free and Independent States.'

Unfortunately most English statesmen of the day failed to foresee the immense help that these rebellious states would one day prove to the world, and dallied on without taking any action. Or perhaps, in spite of Lord Chatham's appeal made as he was dying, they were not much interested.

5th July. Until after 1752 (when the new-style calendar was introduced) this was Midsummer Day. It is well known that Oberon, Titania, and all the other beings responsible for the mysteries and magic of its eve complied with the wishes of George II, the Earl of Macclesfield, and a Mr. Bradby, who engineered the change, and altered their enchantments to the new date.

7th July 1907. The first race of the Brooklands Automobile Club was held on its new track.

This, cut in the quiet Surrey countryside, was the first of many—concrete, dirt, ash—around which mechanical devices, from motor-cycles to mechanical hares, journey at great speed and with immense noise to entertain the people.

14th July 1865. At 1.40 p.m. Edward Whymper and his party achieved the conquest of the Matterhorn. 'Hurrah!' Whymper wrote. 'Not a footstep could be seen'—his Italian rivals, who had started out earlier, were defeated. A possible epoch-maker in the history of mountaineering.

18th July 1817. Wrath would fall on the compiler's head from innumerable otherwise peaceful people if he failed to mention that on this day Miss Austen died at Winchester whither she had gone for change of air and scenery. They will already know that she was born on 16th December 1775 at the parsonage of Steventon in Hampshire; that *Pride and Prejudice*, the first of her novels to be published, was not issued until 1811, long after it was written; and that during her life she preferred anonymity.

19th July 1588. Beacons blazed to signal the arrival in the Channel of Philip of Spain's armada. One hundred and twenty-nine great vessels carried some 20,000 invasion troops. Philip, as do most invaders, thought that a faction of the English (in this case the Catholics) would support him, but found instead an immense wave of loyalty to the throne. The usual hurried preparations took place, and great amateur armies and fleets were collected. But our small navy, commanded by Lord High Admiral Howard of Effingham, who had under him the most brilliant mariners of the age, such as Drake, Hawkins, and Frobisher, was so skilfully and daringly used that, when engaged on the 21st, the heavy Spaniards were utterly perplexed and quite unable to destroy us. From that moment their plans went awry and, continually harried by vicious, accurate attacks and bemused by ploys and stratagems, their disaster was completed by a storm.

21st July 1928. Again femininity demands an entry in the month. In this year died Dame Ellen Terry, whom we include as representative of the great actresses. She was born in Coventry into a family of actors, on 27th February 1847. Her fame, skill, and charm are recorded by many writers of her day. From her first appearance on the stage in 1856 she acted plays whose authors ranged from Shakespeare to Shaw, with hundreds—good, bad, and indifferent —in between.

24th July 1909. At 5.12 a.m. Louis Blériot landed his aircraft on North Fall Meadow, near Dover Castle. He had made the first power-driven crossing of the Channel through the air. A little machine, weighing not much more than four hundredweight, and driven by a twenty-five-horse-power petrol engine, had, by flying the twenty-two miles in thirty-seven minutes, shown that from henceforth man could wilfully approach Britain otherwise than by sea.

The poet's prophecy of 1731 had been realized by a Frenchman in a machine of French design and manufacture, and was to be put into effect:

> England, so long mistress of the sea,
> Where winds and waves confess her sovereignty,
> Her later triumphs yet on high shall bear
> And reign, the sovereign of the conquered air.

25th July 1603. At our invitation James VI of Scotland was crowned James I of England. At his coronation in Westminster Abbey he sat on the stone of Scone which, with the crown jewels, had been stolen from Scotland by Edward I in 1296. The Scots had then prophesied that wherever the sacred stone went a Scottish king would one day rule. Although we have often engaged Scots to manage our affairs to the advantage of both nations, we have never repeated the request that they should send us a king.

27th July 1948. The Thames water bus service between Putney and Greenwich was inaugurated. On a bright morning Miss Patricia Roc, as the first ticket holder, walked down a gangway lined by watermen dressed in the scarlet livery worn by winners of Doggett's Coat and Badge, and took her place on the first trip—a modest, pleasant, and suitable event with which to conclude our July anniversaries.

THE POET

English literature and English poetry rather forget July. Statistically we can show this by a reference to the *Oxford Dictionary of Quotations*, which has only four entries in its index, and one of these is Byron's:

> The English winter—ending in July
> To recommence in August.

The four quotations are but a handful compared with those for the months that stimulate the glands of poets, who then celebrate (and name) them in song. Or perhaps it is because the best rhyme to July is 'fly'—and that was worn out long since in ancient doggerel about cuckoos and bees.

Statistics, however, don't prove much. Internal evidence soon shows that quite a lot of poetry is *about* July, even if it doesn't advertise the month. For instance, I think it was during July, or certainly very late in June, that Tennyson's Maud came into the garden.

As escape from town to the country is the great theme for the month, we can suspect Cowley's wish for a small house and large garden to be away from 'the crowd and buzz and murmurings, of this great hive the city' to be a Julian sentiment. The Caroline Thomas Randolph's expression of Mr. Chambers's claustrophobia in his *Ode to Master Anthony Stafford to hasten him into the Country* can certainly come here:

> Come, spur away,
> I have no patience for a longer stay,
>   But must go down
> And leave the chargeable noise of this great town:
>   I will the country see,
>   Where old simplicity,
>   Though hid in gray,
>   Doth look more gay,
> Than foppery in plush and scarlet clad.
>   Farewell, you city wits, that are
>   Almost at civil war—
> 'Tis time that I grow wise, when all the world grows mad.

>   .   .   .   .   .

>   There from the tree
> We 'll cherries pluck, and pick the strawberry;
>   And every day
> Go see the wholesome country girls make hay,
>   Whose brown hath lovelier grace
>   Than any painted face
>   That I do know
>   Hyde Park can show:
> Where I had rather gain a kiss than meet
>   (Though some of them in greater state
>   Might court my love with plate)
> The beauties of the Cheap, and wives of Lombard Street.

>   .   .   .   .   .

Ours is the sky,
Where at what fowl we please our hawk shall fly:
Nor will we spare
To hunt the crafty fox or timorous hare;
But let our hounds run loose
In any ground they 'll choose;
The buck shall fall,
The stag, and all.
Our pleasures must from their own warrants be,
For to my Muse, if not to me,
I 'm sure all game is free:
Heaven, earth, are all but parts of her great royalty.

And when we mean
To taste of Bacchus' blessings now and then,
And drink by stealth
A cup of two to noble Barkley's health,
I 'll take my pipe and try
The Phrygian melody;
Which he that hears,
Lets through his ears
A madness to distemper all the brain:
Then I another pipe will take
And Doric music make,
To civilize with graver notes our wits again.

From Arcady, before the Roundheads and Cavaliers fought and trampled
in it, we can move to a countryside where nymphs and shepherds have given
way to more pedestrian and industrious peasants, with a good moral outlook,
and trim cottages having their useful gardens around them. Such the
virtuous 'Swan of Bignor,' Charlotte Smith, describes:

The cottage garden, most for use designed,
Is not of beauty destitute. The vine
Mantles the little casement, and the briar
Drops fragrant dew among the July flowers;
And pansies rayed and freaked, with mottled pinks,
Grow among balm, and rosemary, and rue;
There honeysuckles flaunt, and roses blow . . .

Rather later the idyllic picture is restored by Mary Russell Mitford's *Written in July 1824*:

> How oft amid the heaped and buried hay,
>   Under the oak's broad shadow deep and strong
>   Have we sate listening to the noonday song
> (If song it were, monotonously gay)
> Which kept along the field, the summer lay
>   Of the grasshopper.   Summer is come in pride
>   Of fruit and flower, garlanded as a bride,
> And crowned with corn, and graced with length of day.
>   But cold is come with her.   We sit not now
> Listening that merry music of the earth
>   Like Ariel 'beneath the blossomed bough';
> But all for chillness round the social hearth
> We cluster—Hark!—a note of kindred mirth
>   Echoes!—Oh, wintry cricket, welcome thou!

The one poem that I can find unambiguously and simply called *July* (although Richard Church has written of the 'chitter of the sparrows' and quietness in *July Sabbath*), is Austin Dobson's *Virelai nouveau*; again the theme is escape to the country:

> Good-bye to the Town!—good-bye!
> Hurrah! for the sea and the sky!
> In the street the flower-girls cry;
> In the street the water-carts ply;
> And a fluter, with features awry,
> Plays fitfully, 'Scots, wha hae'—
> And the throat of that fluter is dry;
> Good-bye to the Town!—good-bye!
>
> And over the roof-tops high
> Comes a waft like a dream of the May;
> And a lady-bird lit on my tie;
> And a cock-chafer came with the tray;
> And a butterfly (no one knows why)
> Mistook my Aunt's cap for a spray;
> And 'next door' and 'over the way'
> The neighbours take wing and fly:
> Hurrah! for the sea and the sky!

> So Phillis, the fawn-footed, hie
> For a hansom! Ere close of the day
> Between us a 'world' must lie—
> Good-bye to the Town—GOOD-BYE!
> Hurrah! for the sea and the sky!

Our picture becoming less idyllic, I do not see why we should not counter the enthusiastic welcome of the cuckoo with Vivian Ellis's valedictory rhymes:

> Come early, Cuckoo, patient bird,
> And on thy three-stringed viol strum;
> Come early, Cuckoo: thou art heard,
> And no man doubts that spring hath come;
> Tune thy two strings and break the third.
>
> Come seldom, Cuckoo, welcome guest
> Who wear'st thy welcome out too soon;
> Usurper of the small bird's nest,
> Thou art well paid for thy one tune.
> Now get thee gone, thou weariest.

I think, too, that as July is above all the month of the cherry at least part of one 'cherry ripe' song should be quoted, and I have chosen Campion's verses:

> There is a garden in her face
> Where roses and white lilies blow;
> A heavenly paradise is that place,
> Wherein all pleasant fruits do flow:
> There cherries grow which none may buy
> Till 'Cherry-ripe' themselves do cry.
>
> Those cherries fairly do enclose
> Of orient pearl a double row,
> Which when her lovely laughter shows,
> They look like rose-buds fill'd with snow;
> Yet them nor peer nor prince can buy
> Till 'Cherry-ripe' themselves do cry. . . .

And Perdita:

> Here's flowers for you;
> Hot lavender, mints, savory, marjoram;

The marigold, that goes to bed wi' the sun,
And with him rises weeping; these are flowers
Of middle summer, and, I think, they are given
To men of middle age.

Perhaps that is it; July, just past the half-way mark of the year, the middle-aged month. No excited expectation of pleasure that may come, and as yet no alarums of the darkness that is now on its way, but a thousand pleasant things and thoughts to take while they are with us.

AUGUST  LEO

AUGUST is the eighth month and has thirty-one days. In the times before January and February were put into the calendar it was Sextilis, the sixth month, with thirty days. This name was still used at the time when Augustus became emperor of Rome, and was his lucky month. So not to be outdone by his predecessor, Julius Caesar, he added another day to make it as long as July, and ordained that it should be known by his name.

For quite a long time it has been our holiday month; the time when the claustrophobia of the townsman can be relieved with due propriety. To do this he moves in great quantities, simultaneously district by district, to a very limited number of towns situated by the sea. Victorian, Edwardian, and neo-Georgian boarding-houses and hotels, dead for much of the year, suddenly revive. Their walls are nearly burst apart by the holiday crowd, whose members conform to a traditional procedure and a rigid time-table. Thus, just after one o'clock on a Sunday not a soul is abroad. The holiday-makers are eating Sunday dinner. The smell, or even aroma, of its preparation has drifted over the streets throughout the morning.

To the well-established styles in architecture of what are called holiday resorts, a newcomer has been added. Prefabricated hutments are assembled to form holiday camps. These provide a most healthy, mass-produced holiday. Not for one moment can one holiday-maker differ in his actions from at least a section of his fellows.

The genteel have other ways of taking a summer holiday. But even these can be classified into quite a small number of categories. For instance, one group migrates to some very little village in Cornwall—where they stay in a very large hotel. And there are those who *never* go away in August.

126

THE WEATHER

Wet and windy weather is by no means uncommon in early August; indeed, north-country farmers by tradition await the Lammas floods. Buchan places his fifth cold spell as lasting from the 6th to the 11th. Not normally our hottest month, yet it holds the record for the longest heat-waves. Buchan found that towards the middle of August, from the 12th to the 15th, there was usually a recurrence of high temperatures and he gives this as his second hot spell. In 1911 the shade temperature at Greenwich rose to 100° F. on the 9th, which is a record for the London district.

Warm nights are a feature of the month. But sunshine and the other virtues usually fall below the average performance of May, June, and July.

Normal temperature is about 58° F.

There have been some famous August thunderstorms. During one that broke on the 2nd in 1879 a peal of thunder was officially timed at Kew Observatory, and found to last twenty minutes without a break.

Old weather sayings for the month are rather contradictory—perhaps that is why few of them are popularly known.

THE HEAVENS

On 21st August the sun leaves Leo and enters Virgo, the Virgin.

FEASTS, FAIRS, AND FESTIVALS

1st August.   Lammas Day.

Lammas Day, or the Gule of August, was one of the great pagan festivals —the festival celebrating the first fruits of harvest. The name derives from Loaf-mass, or consecration of loaves made from the season's first corn.

Formerly it was occasionally a custom to let land from Lady until Lammas. It was therefore a day on which rent was paid—sometimes partly in kind in new wheat of the season.

The Church has recently revived the spirit of the occasion, and transferred to the first Sunday in August a first-fruits offering with a new form of service.

5th August.   St. Oswald.

He was a Christian king of Northumbria who was killed in 642 while fighting against Penda, pagan king of Mercia.

Patron saint of the church at Grasmere, the ancient rush-bearing ceremony is still carried out on the Saturday nearest his festival.

12th August.   Mitcham Fair.

This still draws crowds when it opens at Three Kings Common as it has done since Elizabeth's day.   She has always been supposed to have granted the fair a charter, but when some years ago a search was made for it it could not be found.

15th August.   The Assumption of the Blessed Virgin Mary.

In both the Norman and Greek Churches, this day is celebrated in remembrance of the corporeal ascent of the Virgin Mary to heaven, which took place in A.D. 45.   The Church of England now prefers to call it the 'Falling Asleep of the Blessed Virgin Mary.'

In medieval times it was the occasion of a famous minstrel's festival at Tutbury Castle in Staffordshire.

24th August.   St. Bartholomew.   Apostle and Martyr.

Tradition imaginatively says that after the death of Christ this apostle carried his mission to 'the Indians'—perhaps Arabia Felix.   His character typifies sincerity.   His symbol, a knife, signifies that he was flayed alive.

We are told that this was once the principal occasion on which the Horn Dance was performed at Abbott's Bromley in Staffordshire.   The dancers carry reindeer's horns.   These are probably older than their mounting, which is of sixteenth-century work.   The origins of the ceremony are obscure and probably ancient.   Yet it has been kept so much alive over the centuries that certain features, such as the dress worn and music now used, are comparatively recent.   It is significant that the patron of the village church is St. Nicholas, whose emblem is a reindeer.   The Horns are now danced later in the year.

In the days before glazing of windows was common St. Bartholomew's was the day of the London printer's wayzgoose. New paper windows were put up. The correctors, ink-makers, and other specialized craftsmen gave money to the ordinary workers or journeymen so that they might feast—let us hope, on roast goose rather than beans!

At Gulval in Cornwall the Festival of the Blessing of the Mead takes place.

31st August.   St. Aidan.

He died on this day in 651. Born in Ireland he became Bishop of Lindisfarne, an island much given to receiving the mortal remains of saints. He wrought many miracles and was a good prophet. One day his oxen were hauling a load of timber when cart and oxen fell from a high rock into the sea.. As they fell Aidan had time to make the sign of the cross so that the whole outfit was able to walk out of the water unharmed.

THE SPORTSMAN

With one exception the sports of August are of rather more interest to the individualist and the participator than to teams and crowds.

On the first, in celebration of the accession of George I to the throne on 1st August 1714 the young watermen of the river Thames row for Doggett's Coat and Badge. The founder of the prizes was Thomas Doggett, a successful actor and an ardent supporter of the Hanoverian cause. Doggett himself designed the orange coat. The badge bears the white horse of Hanover. The race was first rowed in 1715, and at his death Doggett left money to perpetuate the award.

August is the month when a number of sporting birds may be shot again, and it is perhaps appropriate to recall the death on 7th August 1853 of Colonel Peter Hawker in his sixty-seventh year. After a wound at Talavera he left the army and devoted the rest of his life to shooting. He is now regarded as the father of shooting as a modern field sport. His *Instructions to Young Sportsmen in all that Relates to Guns and Shooting* remains a classic, although breech loading long ago ousted the muzzle-loader of his day. His favourite quarry was partridge.

On the 1st August wild-duck shooting, mallard and teal, comes into season. Mallard is our most abundant resident duck, and is increased by migration during the winter. Teal is our smallest, and though some are resident, large numbers begin to arrive during the month. On the same day quail and snipe shooting may start. The quail is our smallest game bird, and is a summer visitor to our islands, travelling in hordes, but during the autumn shooting season the birds form into a small family group called a bevy. Many quail leave in October. Snipe is a specialist's sport. The quarry lives mostly in wild and difficult places, as often as not boggy into the bargain. There are three kinds, two of which are fairly abundant; the common or full snipe, which when disturbed rises with a darting, zigzag flight, and the smaller or jack-snipe, which makes short straight flights.

All these four birds provide fine sport, and their shooting has become particularly associated with the modern sportsmen-naturalists.

On the 1st, our calendars tell us, it is also permissible to shoot land-rail and wood-pigeons. The first is better known as the corncrake or grass-quail —a common summer visitor until modern farming upset its habits. Now its rasping voice, once so familiar, is a rare sound. Wood-pigeons to-day are such a pest that they are officially destroyed on every possible occasion.

On the 12th begins the pursuit of *Lagopus scoticus scoticus*. The reader may think that the printer has inadvertently duplicated the last word, but it is only a little trick of the ornithologist by which he distinguishes the red from other kinds of grouse. This little bird of the northern moorlands provides the most superior sort of shooting. It is a difficult quarry for the sportsman, both because it dwells in wild and spacious places, often on magnificent estates, and because it needs good marksmanship. In an even more northerly terrain and on higher ground, the ptarmigan or muirfowl, somewhat similar to the grouse, is also in season. Neither may be shot on Christmas Day or Sunday.

On the 20th black grouse or black game may be shot except in Somerset, Devon, and the New Forest, where the opening day is 1st September. It is another moorland or hill-living bird belonging to a different genus from the red grouse. The male is known as the blackcock, the female as the grey hen.

The shooting man's August almanac concludes with the 31st of the month, after which he may no longer shoot the bustard.

One invariably refers to shooting, but there are still a few who follow the more ancient sport of pursuing some of these game-birds with hawks.

Of other field sports cub hunting begins during August, and man is permitted to kill at least the young of the fox in a gentlemanly way—for the fox, alas, is given no close season by law.

Until recent times we should have ended there, but now, while the last calm days of really sporting cricket meander on (there is the Canterbury Festival which combines cricket with the drama), the roars are heard of the multitude cheering on their local teams in the Football League competitions.

The Football League came into being largely owing to the energies of a Mr. McGregor, after a meeting at the Royal Hotel, Manchester, on 17th April 1888. Football was controlled by the Football Association, and was originally largely an amateur's game. It so increased in popularity, and professionalism became so universal, that it was necessary to bring into some organization the thousand or so clubs then existing—quite apart from legislating for the conduct of the game. Thus the League was formed from clubs playing under the Football Association's rules. The championship of the First Division of the League and the Football Association's Cup are the two highest honours a club can achieve. The first is, of course, based on points awarded in games throughout the season; the second is a knock-out competition.

There are now between 30,000 and 40,000 clubs connected with the League.

THE NATURALIST

August, the month of large dragon-flies coursing backwards and forwards over land and water (even in the middle of cities), of peaches, pink heaths, of strange bulbous plants such as *Tigridia*, and gladiolus—these are a few incidents in a quiet month when all now steadily develops towards fruition.

To consider dragon-flies first. Ranging from fragile demoiselles to the stately and handsome hawkers, these harmless creatures living on insects have collected names such as horse-stingers, devil's darning needles, flying adders, and snake-feeders. Their scientific names are worse. The best we have are *Aeshna* and *Agrion*, but *Gomphus*, *Somatochlora*, and *Cordulegaster* prove that there has been something wrong with the experts who have named these flying bits of enamel, coursing, darting, and twisting, borne on matchless reticulated wings.

Peaches and nectarines, believed to have come originally from ancient

China, have befitting and dignified names, starting with the botanist's *Prunus Persica*, which covers them all, to the gardener's peregrine, crimson galande, early grosse mignonne, and kestrel for peaches, and cardinal, Dryden, and elruge for nectarines.

We must return to the water-side, where the big brown *Aeshna* lives and hunts. There is far more to see there than in the dark dried woods, or the cut and grazed fields. The bur-reed, with spikes of globular flowers, the small males above the larger females, the branching inflorescence of the water plantain, the flowering rush with umbels of pink flowers, and most showy of all, the purple loose-strife, will all still be blooming. Teachers of botany love this last, because it bears several different kinds of flower in which the pistil and stamens vary, with the result that there are eighteen different ways in which it can be fertilized. In damp places, too, the mints will be flowering. One writer has gone so far as to call August 'the month of the mints.'

Aeshna dragon-fly on Bur-reed

Though the water-side remains fascinating, August is, above all, the month when moorland and peaty upland bogs come into their own. Ling, bell-heather, and the other heaths are in full flower. In damp places the lovely pink-flowered bush, sweet gale, is seen. The little herb, grass of Parnassus, is also to be found. It is entirely unlike a grass, belongs to the Saxifragaceae, but doesn't look like our garden saxifrages. This is another plant with an ingenious device to ensure cross fertilization, the anthers uncurling themselves at the appropriate moment in an ingenious manner.

In dry grassy places—neglected lawns in particular—and on hillsides grazed by sheep and rabbits, a whole party of brassy little composites comes into its own—hawkweeds, hawkbits, hawk's-beard, and cat's-ear. They are peculiarly irritating to the gardener—they thrive and produce a mass of seed in dry seasons when the grass goes brown. The larger members of the party, apart from their metallic colour, are quite handsome. One, the umbellate hawkweed, sometimes colonizes railway embankments and turns dry, brown banks into a sheet, if not of gold, of very shiny brass. Other grassland plants now are the little eyebright or *Euphrasia*, a gem seen through a glass—and the odd-looking yellow rattle. They are interesting to botanists as partial parasites on the grass among which they grow.

Seaweed and Shells

The hedgerow flower of the month is undoubtedly the greater bindweed or 'wild convolvulus.' Handsome as are its large hanging bells and interesting as is its root system, few plants bring greater despair to the gardener wishing to eradicate it.

At the seaside we usually find all the plants of the dry grass-land, and even of the heaths, above the shore on cliffs and hills. In the south the common pink centaury (not to be confused with *Centaurea* of botanists, the name for knapweed) is a pretty little plant usually abundant in short turf in the 'rough' of golf-links. On the upper part of cliffs thyme will often be growing. Of plants peculiar to the seaside, samphire, sea-lavender, sea-holly, and sea-plantain are but a few of those that will now be found in flower. On the shore itself there are the enchantments of seaweeds and shells.

Trees have lost their shine apart from those on the untidy and irregular second growth known as 'Lammas shoots.' In London parks the catalpas or Indian bean-trees will be bearing panicles of white foxglove flowers.

Rather surprisingly these are followed by fruits very much like an ordinary runner bean. But, particularly in towns, trees are beginning to show signs of wear from weather, fungus (the dirty spots on sycamore leaves), and caterpillars. These 'signals of autumn' are well described by Anthony Collett:[1] 'In town and country alike leaves and clusters of leaves fretted through the long calm days by summer caterpillars come tossing to earth in the August rain and wind. The same winds cast down a sprinkling of the caterpillars which have caused the decay. . . . The long green caterpillars of the buff-tip moth, with their parallel black lines, are among the commonest of these living windfalls. . . . The large horned caterpillars of various hawkmoths also fall now and then from tall trees in the August winds. Even under the lime-trees in Kensington Gardens . . . a lime-hawk caterpillar fell once among the withered leaves.'

We started by mentioning some garden plants, but August is really a quiet month for the gardener. The early autumn flowers—chrysanthemums, dahlias, and Michaelmas daisies—are on their way, but not yet at their height. Phlox, however, may be at their best, with their own peculiar scent that belongs to late summer and which, when first noticed, brings home the now undeniable fact that high summer is once again in the past. Few shrubs bloom, but there is one lovely exception which is rapidly finding its way into gardens—*Eucryphia*, from the southern hemisphere, bearing white blossoms centred by a boss of golden stamens.

We now notice that mixed flocks of the smaller birds are working the hedgerows. They consist predominantly of young birds—tits, warblers, gold-crests, tree-creepers, and finches. One day we realize that the swifts have gone, this time for good—the first real sign that the passage of birds, some to the north and others to the south, which slows down but scarcely ceases for more than a month in the year, is in full swing again. The older cuckoos probably went in July, leaving the young to follow. Wood-warblers, nightjars, and red-backed shrikes also move away. Our coasts see the first of migrating sanderling, stint, and dunlin. Of ducks many are on the move, the drakes gay and in the air again, recovered from their eclipse.

Birds are now very quiet. Hedge-sparrow, yellow-hammer, stock-dove, wood-pigeon, and starling are among the undistinguished few that can be

[1] *The Changing Year.*

heard. During the month a robin may remind us, only too convincingly, that another autumn is not far away.

Of animal life I have a note that young blindworms and adders are born. This allows us to end August with a holiday question. Do mother adders swallow their young when alarmed? There are as nearly as many different answers as there are experts.

ANNIVERSARIES OF EVENTS, EPOCHS, AND RECORDS

1st August 1749. 'Rule, Britannia,' an ode in the masque *Alfred*, by James Thomson and David Mallet, with music by Thomas Arne, was first performed in the gardens of Cliefden House, Maidenhead, before the Prince of Wales.

1st August 1834. From this day all slaves in the British Empire were free.

2nd August 1788. Of our handful of great painters we commemorate on this day the most delightful and charming, Thomas Gainsborough, R.A., who died in London from 'a malignant wen,' which he had first noticed as he sat watching the trial of Warren Hastings. A lover of life, music, and the countryside, he made his living as a portrait painter—in this, as in practically every way, he was a complete contrast to his contemporary Reynolds—and for love painted landscapes which remained unsold. He left but little property on his death.

10th August 1675. Charles II laid the 'foundation stone of Time itself'—Greenwich Observatory. The building was designed by Sir Christopher Wren, and John Flamsteed was appointed first Astronomer Royal.

10th August 1575. Peter Bales, writing master, wrote the Lord's Prayer, the Decalogue, the Creed, and some minor items on a circle the size of a penny. It was framed in gold, covered with crystal, presented to Queen Elizabeth, and easily qualifies as our August record-maker.

12th August 1827. We must include at least one of our English mystics, and we could not do better than commemorate William Blake, who died on this day, and whose drawings and, to a less extent, writings are now most popular. His father kept a hosier's shop in Golden Square, where he was born on 28th

November 1757. As a child he showed a talent for design, and an interest in works of art which was encouraged by his parents, though he received little formal education. He lived his life in London, and was not very successful at looking after his worldly affairs. He devised a system of printing plates from his drawings; he was, therefore, author, illustrator, printer, and publisher of nearly all his books. Most of his work is quite unmistakable—lyrical songs, rambling philosophy, mystic religion, and drawings which writhe with energy and muscle and can be called unique with accuracy and without offence.

13th August 1910. Florence Nightingale died at her home in Park Lane, London. She was born at Florence on 12th May 1820. In about 1844 she started her visits and studies of hospitals on the Continent. Following the appalling treatment of our sick and wounded she offered her services to the War Office on 14th October 1854. They were accepted. The rest of the story and the effect of this determined woman on hospital administration and the art of nursing is history.

22nd August 1485. Richard III was defeated and killed by Henry Tudor at the battle of Bosworth Field, fought near Leicester. Henry took the crown that Richard hid under a hawthorn-tree, and was made king. Thus ended the years of misery, murder, and warfare known as the Wars of the Roses. History books used to say that the occasion marked the end of the Middle Ages.

22nd August 1715. George I, the Prince and Princess of Wales, and a large party of nobility were rowed in barges from Whitehall to Limehouse. The procession was accompanied by music as it progressed slowly along the river; the occasion is, indeed, recalled only because Handel wrote for it his ever-popular *Water Music*. The pretty legend that it was written to reinstate the composer in the royal esteem—which, of course, it succeeded in doing—is unhappily groundless.

. As the royal barge came upstream in the evening houses on the banks were illuminated, shipping had lanterns hung in the rigging, and crowded boats of spectators attended the party. Cannons were fired continually both during the day and at night.

137

24th August 1847. 'Mr. Jones of Grosvenor Street performed an extraordinary operation in dental surgery by the aid of ether. He extracted seven teeth from a young lady in delicate health, who was utterly unconscious of any pain.'

25th August. To-day's anniversaries all mark events in the history of the alarming progress of our mechanical age.

The first is concerned with the development of power from coal by steam, for in 1819 died James Watt, who, by adding a condenser and other fitments to the existing crude mechanisms, produced the modern steam engine. This soon became and for long remained almost the universal source of power, and soon resulted in a network of mechanical transport covering this and other countries.

Watt, the son of an unsuccessful merchant in Greenock, was born 19th January 1736. He did not develop his engine until he met Matthew Boulton, proprietor of an engineering works at Soho, then near Birmingham. The partnership was immensely successful, and was responsible for the production of many ingenuities. In early and middle life Watt was a gloomy, despondent, and seedy man—Boulton was just the opposite. However, in old age he cheered up, and was 'an alert, kind, benevolent old man, his talents and fancy overflowing.'

We next come to the development of electricity, which became complementary to and in many cases superseded steam. Michael Faraday died on this day in 1867. He was born on 22nd February 1791, the son of a Yorkshire blacksmith, who migrated to Newington in Surrey. Chemist, electrician, and philosopher, he discovered on 29th August 1831 that an electric current can induce another in a different circuit—'Think I have got hold of a good thing, but can't say,' he wrote. The 'good thing' ultimately grew into the dynamo; from it the electrical industry speedily developed.

Finally we come to an anniversary in air transport. At 9.10 on the morning of this day in 1919 a wartime de Havilland 4 biplane crudely converted for civilian purposes took off from Hounslow Heath to inaugurate the first regular overseas air service between London and Paris. The pilot was Lieutenant E. H. Lawford; the load a journalist, some newspapers, grouse, and Devonshire cream. The plane touched down at Le Bourget after a flight of two and a quarter hours.

26th August, 55 B.C.   Julius Caesar, with a handful of Romans, first set foot in England—on the coast of Kent between Walmer and Deal.   The landing, though no more than a first reconnaisance, can justly be claimed as marking the start of a not unimportant epoch.

THE POET

> Can you tell me where has hid her
>   Pretty Maid July? . . .
>
> She has muddied the day's oozes
>   With her petulant feet;
> Scared the clouds that floated,
>   As sea-birds they were,
> Slow on the coerule
>   Lulls of the air,
> Lulled on the luminous
>   Levels of air . . .

With these lines from Francis Thompson's *July Fugitive* we may regret her, and then welcome August by quoting Dryden's version of Horace:

> The sun is in the Lion mounted high;
>   The Syrian star
>   Barks from afar,
> And with his sultry breath infects the sky;
> The ground below is parch'd, the heav'ns above us fry.
>   The shepherd drives his fainting flock
>   Beneath the covert of a rock
>   And seeks refreshing rivulets nigh.
>   The Sylvans to their shades retire,
> Those very shades and streams new shades and streams require,
> And want a cooling breeze of wind to fan the raging fire.

For an August landscape we have, from the *Shepherd's Calendar*, Clare's

> Harvest approaches with its busy day;
> The wheat tans brown, and barley bleaches grey;
> In yellow garb the oatland intervenes,
> And tawny glooms the valley throng'd with beans.

139

Silent the village grows—wood-wandering dreams
Seem not so lonely as its quiet seems;
Doors are shut up as on a winter's day,
And not a child about them lies at play;
The dust that winnows 'neath the breeze's feet
Is all that stirs about the silent street:
Fancy might think that desert-spreading Fear
Had whisper'd terrors into Quiet's ear,
Or plundering armies past the place had come
And drove the last inhabitants from home.
The fields now claim them, where a motley crew
Of old and young their daily tasks pursue. . . .

Or Matthew Arnold's Oxfordshire harvesting scene in *The Scholar Gipsy*:

Here, where the reaper was at work of late—
In this high field's dark corner, where he leaves
His coat, his basket, and his earthen cruse,
And in the sun all morning binds the sheaves,
Then here, at noon, comes back his stores to use—
Here will I sit and wait,
While to my ears from uplands far away
The bleating of the folded flocks is borne,
With distant cries of reapers in the corn—
All the live murmur of a summer's day.

Screen'd in this nook o'er the high, half-reap'd field,
And here till sun-down, shepherd! will I be.
Through the thick corn the scarlet poppies peep,
And round green roots and yellowing stalks I see
Pale blue convolvulus in tendrils creep;
And air-swept lindens yield
Their scent, and rustle down their perfumed showers
Of bloom on the bent grass where I am laid,
And bower me from the August sun with shade;
And the eye travels down to Oxford's towers.

An odd poem called *The Month of August* is by Mary Leapor (1722–46) who,
Mr. Iolo Williams tells us, was a cook-maid and the daughter of a gardener.

It consists of an argument between Sylvanus, a courtier, who is all for formality
and tidy gardens, and Phillis, a country maid, who is a supporter of nature
and agriculture.   This is typical of the argument:

SYLVANUS

But see, to emulate those cheeks of thine,
On yon fair tree the blushing nect'rines shine:
Beneath their leaves the ruddy peaches glow,
And the plump figs compose a gallant show,
With gaudy plums see yonder boughs recline,
And ruddy pears in yon espalier twine.
There humble dwarfs in pleasing order stand,
Whose golden product seems to court thy hand.

PHILLIS

In vain you tempt me, while our orchard bears
Long-keeping russets, lovely Cath'rine pears,
Pearmains and codlings, wheaten plums enow,
And the black damsons load the bending bough.
No pruning-knives our fertile branches tease,
While yours must grow but as their masters please.
The grateful trees our mercy well repay,
And rain us bushels at the rising day.

There is also Thomas Hardy's little morality, *An August Midnight*:

A shaded lamp and a waving blind,
And the beat of a clock from a distant floor:
On this scene enter—winged, horned, and spined—
A longlegs, a moth, and a dumbledore;
While 'mid my page there idly stands
A sleepy fly, that rubs its hands . . .

Thus meet we five, in this still place,
At this point of time, at this point in space.
—My guests besmear my new-penned line,
Or bang at the lamp and fall supine.
'God's humblest they!' I muse.   Yet why?
They know Earth-secrets that know not I.

And finally Laurence Binyon's *August Weeds*:

I wandered between woods
On a grassy down, when still
Clouds hung after rain
Over hollow and hill;

The blossom-time was over,
The singing throats dumb,
And the year's coloured ripeness
Not yet come.

And all at unawares,
Surprising the stray sight,
Ran straight into my heart
Like a beam, delight.

Negligent weeds ravelled
The green edge of the copse,
Whitely, dimly, sparkling
With a million drops.

And sudden fancy feigned
What strange beauty would pass
Did but a shiver of wind
Tremble through the grass,

Shaking the poised, round crops
Spilled and softly rolled
A-glitter from the ragwort's
Roughened gold;

From the rusted scarlet
Of tall sorrel seed,
And fretted tufts, frost-gray,
Of the silver-weed,

And from the purple-downed thistle
Towering dewy over
Yellow-cupped spurge
And the drenched, sweet clover.

But all were motionless:
Not one breath shed
Those little pale pearls
That an elf might thread

Under a fading moon
By an old thorn-tree
For the witching throat
Of Nìmuë.

SEPTEMBER   VIRGO

SEPTEMBER is now the ninth month, with thirty days. Like the remaining months of the year its name comes from the number of the month in the first Roman calendar—in this case, *septem*, seven. How the suffix *ber* came to be added no one seems to know.

Gerstmonath or barley month was its Anglo-Saxon equivalent.

It falls at the time when over the greater part of our island the grain harvest is gathered in. Many odd practices and superstitions collected round this ancient and vital undertaking, once so precariously dependent on the weather. They began to die as machinery replaced the skill of man's hand and tractors the sweat of his body. Now that a roaring monster heads the procession of the combine harvester followed by its appurtenances, gobbling up the grain between showers, they will doubtless disappear entirely.

The first to go when machinery came in were the Lord and Lady of the Harvest, who set the pace of the old hand-reapers with their sickles. The cutter of the last sheaf on the farm was doomed to ill luck. Sickles were thrown at it, and other ingenious devices contrived so that it should not be reaped by a sickle held in the hand. But when down it was treated with grave respect, for it was now a woman—Ceres herself, the corn spirit. Dressed and decorated, known as the Corn Maiden or Kern Baby and by other local names, she was prominently placed at the Mell Supper or Harvest Home. This was given by the farmer to celebrate the clearing of his fields—a 'mell' because his family and workers all mixed together. The harvest supper still lingers on, indeed, it is being revived in some places, but generally has died out.

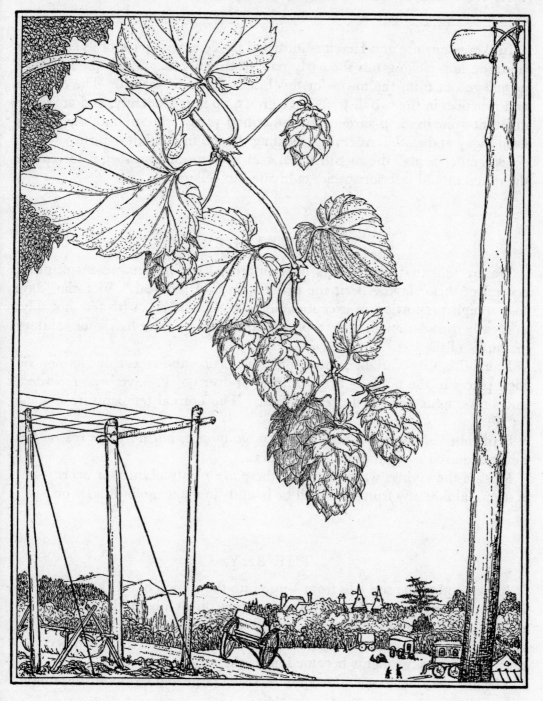

In Worcestershire and Herefordshire and in Kent, with parts of its adjoining counties, hop-picking fills the early part of the month. Many thousands of people go out from the towns for this brief and hectic season. The customs and practices in the two districts have grown up independently, and are quite different—one has hop-gardens, the other hop-yards. But in both the pickers form a gay and riotous assembly, tackling the job in a holiday spirit.

September is also the month when real field mushrooms begin to replace the different and inferior species cultivated in cellars.

THE WEATHER

We are told that Septembers have improved during the present century, several of them having been the driest month of the year. Victorian days had a high proportion of exceptionally wet Septembers, with few hot days and early frosts—though it must be admitted that we have had some salutary examples of the last.

Rainfall is very variable, snow sometimes falls, and is not uncommon on high places in the north. Temperatures of over 90° F. have been recorded, and on occasion several degrees of frost. The normal temperature is some 55° F.

September is, therefore, an unpredictable month, but for some reason has never acquired a reputation for fickleness.

Most of the sayings warn us that if there are plenty of nuts, or acorns—or, it seems, almost any fruit—we shall be bound 'to make up for it later on.'

THE SKY

In September the sun falls from Virgo into the section of the sky dominated by Libra, the Scales. The transition occurs on or about the 22nd of the month. This gives us the autumn equinox. Day and night are again equal and the sun rises due east and sets due west. Once passed the moon becomes mistress of the sky; nights become longer than days.

The full moon nearest to the equinox, rising large and red soon after sunset, is known as the harvest moon.   To-day it is considered to be merely a coincidence that by this behaviour the hours of light are prolonged just at a busy season for farmers; earlier generations were, perhaps, a little wiser.

FEASTS, FAIRS, AND FESTIVALS

1st September.   St. Giles.

Although this saint has no direct link with our country, his festival should be remembered if only because of his popularity as a patron of churches. Tradition says that he was a rich Athenian, who gave all his belongings to the poor, and then retired to live in a cave in a desert.   A hind used to visit him and provide him with milk.   Once when hunting the King of France inadvertently shot an arrow into the hermit, who, that he might better mortify the flesh, refused aid, and remained a cripple all his life.   Thus he became the patron of cripples, with the heaven-directed hind as his symbol.

St. Giles Fair is held at Oxford on the Monday after this day.   The traditional pitch is in St. Giles and Magdalen Streets.   St. John's College still takes the fees from the stall-holders.

3rd September.

Once this was the day when the Lord Mayor of London proclaimed Bartholomew Fair.   The proclamation included numerous regulations to ensure fair trading with full weight and measure.   The fair lasted three days exclusive of proclamation day.

From the earliest times it seems to have been famous for its side shows. Ben Jonson wrote of them.   In 1814 we read of 'the Fireproof Lady, Madame Girardelli, who put melted lead in her mouth and spat it out marked with her teeth; she washed her hands not only in boiling lead, but boiling oil and aqua-fortis.'

It was held at Smithfield and disappeared in the eighteen-fifties after seven and a half centuries of life.

4th September.   St. Cuthbert.

Cuthbert was Bishop of Lindisfarne in the seventh century.   Long after his death, during lulls in the great storms that rage along the coasts of

Northumberland, he could be heard at work forging beads. The hammering of the saint is no longer audible, but the beads are still found. They are a peculiar type of fossil.

14th September. Holy Cross Day.

On this day is recalled the appearance of the cross in a noon sky to Constantine the Great, Emperor of Rome in the third century and founder of Constantinople.

Two old customs are associated with it. School children used to be given a holiday so that they might go nutting, and the king's huntsmen were allowed to hunt a free buck for themselves in Richmond Park.

Michaelmas Daisies (painted lady, red admiral, and hover-fly)

19th September.

Once a famous fair, connected with the university, was held at Stourbridge, near Cambridge. In the seventeenth century its fame attracted visitors from London. Later its popularity waned, but the enthusiasm of a celebrated eighteenth-century squire, Jacob Butler, kept it going. He used to invite the giants and dwarfs to lunch with him.

On the Sunday nearest this day the ceremony 'clipping the church' takes place at Painswick in Gloucestershire. Children join hands and form a ring all round the church, and then advance and retreat three times. The villagers eat 'puppy-dog pies'—now round cakes with a china dog inside. Other features of the occasion, which is certainly very old, persuade some antiquarians that it is a direct descendant of the *Lupercalia*—Painswick was a Roman settlement.

21st September.   St. Matthew.   Apostle, Evangelist, and Martyr.

Traditionally known as the author of the first gospel, there is very little recorded about this saint.   As an evangelist he is shown in old pictures seated beside an angel who dictates to him; as an apostle he holds a purse of money (since he was a publican), a spear, or a carpenter's rule.

English tradition seems not to have accumulated around him.

29th September.   St. Michael and All Angels.   Michaelmas.

Michael is first of all angels.   It was he who was in command when the rebel angels were driven out of heaven.   A handsome but severe-looking young man, he is shown wearing shining armour, his wings folded behind him, a lance in his hand with which he fights a dragon.

His day seems to have become associated with the slaughter of stock fattened during the summer—geese on the grass that no longer grows, and the cottager's pig for curing as winter stores.

The feast has also given its name to the numerous gay forms and hybrids of the *Aster* family which flower about this time.

The day was once quite generally chosen for the election of mayors and magistrates with attendant celebrations.   For instance, they were chosen at Kidderminster on the Monday following Michaelmas.   Afterwards the day seems to have become a holiday and several thousand people assembled in the centre of the town to receive apples thrown down to them by the householders and officials from the upper rooms.

THE SPORTSMAN

I think that we should give pride of place to football, both Association, although this has now somehow precociously strayed into August, and Rugby, for September is really their month; they replace cricket, lawn tennis, bowls, and all those other ball games which practically disappear at the end of August, when our finer turf becomes too soft and sticky.

Football—and it must be admitted by soccer enthusiasts that their code, prohibiting the use of hands, is quite a new idea—is a very ancient game. Some say that it originated in an early rite to bring down rain; certainly many strange forms are still played on Shrove Tuesday, whose origins were not in sport as we know it.

One of the earliest accounts of football in its simplest form, possession of and attack on a goal, is found in 1175. A hundred years later professionalism—at least to the extent of cash reward for services—is recorded.

Teal (drake)

Modern football began at public schools, and first became famous from *Tom Brown's Schooldays* in 1857. The first school rules were drawn up at Rugby in 1846; the first 'foreign' match was played in 1867. Soon other schools took to it, though one or two remained faithful to their original games. Adult clubs were then formed.

In 1871 the English Rugby Union came into being, prepared rules, and directed the conduct of the game. Except in a few localities rugger remains a game played by schools and small clubs of amateur enthusiasts.

Association football, the junior and more specialized game, is believed to have originated at Cambridge University. It was primarily an amateur's game when the Football Association was formed—from which, of course, it gains the name Association, shortened to soccer. That was after a meeting at a public-house called the Freemasons' Arms on 26th October 1863.

The popularity of the game spread, professionalism practically ousted the amateur from first-class games (the Corinthians battled on nobly), and to-day the game has become primarily an entertainment of the masses. Immense sums of money are involved in its conduct, and fortunes may be won on its results.

The hockey season also begins. This game is played by comparatively few; perhaps because women join in with men and male injuries are rather frequent. It is a modern game that has developed almost entirely since the eighteen-eighties—the Hockey Association was formed in 1886.

From the first of the month *Perdix*, the partridge, may be shot, except on Sunday or Christmas Day. This bird lives in farming land pretty well all over our island; partridge shooting is an old and popular sport. On the same day black game shooting comes into season in Somerset, Devon, and the New Forest.

Sometime about the middle of the month other hunting ends.

On 24th September 1776 the first St. Leger sweepstake was run on Cantley Common, Doncaster. It was proposed by Lieutenant-General St. Leger (the race did not take his name until 1778) and won by Lord Rockingham's Alabaculia. The Doncaster meeting and this race, the fifth and final classic of the year, are still held during the middle part of the month.

September is known as 'the mare's month'—fillies being out of condition during the summer, but coming on again in autumn.

For the rest trout and char fishing end with the month; the ardent trout fisherman must now be content with grayling.

THE NATURALIST

This month we can be in no doubt, however warm and sunny the weather, that summer is ending. Everywhere we notice fruits—tufts of down on the composites, berries in the hedgerow, pears and apples in the orchard—all proper to autumn and winter. Even in this month greengages will have ripened, plums will be at their best, some apples will be ready, and Williams's Bon Chrétien pear will be picked.

The woodsides and hedgerows are a tangle. We have rose hips, thorn haws, and hazel nuts; below them are the red berries of cuckoo-pint. The whole mass is overgrown by twiners and stragglers, all in fruit. In the dense mass two are almost universal—blackberry and black bryony.

Blackberries—they must be eaten before Michaelmas Day when the devil gets into them—have long been studied by botanists who loved to argue over the varying forms that they found. Genetecists have now found that attempts to reach finality by the older methods of botanical classification may only lead to bewilderment. The extraordinary variation within the group of plants known as *Rubus fruticosus* is due to hybridization and involved complexities of fertilization and seed production. It will be remembered that the long shoots of blackberries generally root when they reach the ground, so that a variation, having once come to maturity, will probably increase and perpetuate itself quite independently of any seed that it produces. Thus we have a 'clone' both originated and propagated by nature; usually nature (man often claims to have helped) does the originating and man (sometimes even impeded by nature) does the propagating.

Black bryony is a much simpler plant to study. It is the sole English member of the yam family, which is largely tropical. The only confusion is in its name. Black applies to the root, not the berry, which is scarlet. It is no relation of white bryony. This has a red or orange berry, and is named from the thick white root which is still called by some English mandrake, and by them is claimed to have the powers of that magic plant. White bryony is plentiful in many places, though it has not the same wide distribution as the last two plants.

On limestone soils hedges will often be mounded over with a mat of the silky tassels of our only clematis. In flower it is called traveller's joy; in seed, old man's beard.

The dearth of wild flowers drives butterflies to our gardens. Buddleias are covered with them. The commonest are the usual whites, red admirals (who love rotting plums even more), tortoiseshells, peacocks, painted ladies, and brimstones. At night many handsome moths come to the flowers. In some years the south coast has invasions of the rare striped hawk-moth, which feeds in the evenings on the nectar of petunias. But however crowded the garden may seem, butterflies and moths decrease in numbers very considerably during the month. Many that we see are about to hibernate.

Ivy flowers provide one of the few sources of food for nectar-sipping insects left among wild plants. Wasps and drone flies in particular swarm around them. Flies, mosquitoes, wasps, hornets, midges, and all the more pestilential, stinging, and irritating of Pandora's horde seem at their most vicious on a warm September day. A cheerful and harmless little fellow who also reaches his highest population this month is the water whirligig beetle.

September is also a month when we see or feel much of some insect-like animals. Droplets from heavy dews cling on to and display the webs that spiders spin over hedges and grass. Many kinds now achieve their maximum population and are busy egg-laying. The frosts will kill off most of them— the common, and now very abundant, garden spider will be one of the first to die when cold weather comes. The large long-legged house spider, *Tegenaria atrica*, in particular seems to be moving noisily about and mildly alarming us during early autumn. The irritating 'harvester,' which burrows into our shin for no good reason, and certainly not to its own benefit, is at its most irritating now, particularly where there are limestone or chalky soils. It would surely be better for everybody if it remained among the stubble and bracken. Those strange, long-legged creatures, superficially spider-like, of the order Opiliones, known as harvestmen, are also often seen. Little is known of them or their way of life.

Woodland and inland birds leave in large numbers. Some nightingales may have left in August, and the rest now follow. Early in the month garden, grasshopper, and reed-warblers, and redstarts leave. Then whitethroats and whinchats. Towards the end we lose willow-warblers, chiff-chaffs, common sandpipers, spotted flycatchers, tree pipits, wheatears, turtle-doves, and yellow wagtails. Swallows and martins congregate, lining telegraph wires and perching on dead trees, ready for their flight.

Arrivals are teal, pintail, jack-snipe, and countless waders. The big grey lag geese, which once bred here much more freely than they now do, fly southward to us. If the weather is bad in northern Europe the first redwing and fieldfare may arrive.

But for the robin and twittering of the accumulating swallows, there is little bird song. Enthusiastic sparrows and wood-pigeons may attempt a final nest.

In the longer nights we may now hear the barking of foxes. The strange (it has well been called peacock-like) yelping of the vixen and the sharp yapping of the dog make an unearthly din.

Other migrations are under way. Some eels, specially dressed in a silver travelling livery, no doubt to match the 'golden lamps in a green night,' start on their way to Bermuda. There, in one little spot in the whole vast ocean, the long fantastic journey completed, they breed.

In the reverse direction salmon and those trout visiting the sea will be entering our river-mouths and making their astonishing climb up to the fresh waters where they spawn.

Of wild flowers heather and the yellow composites are among the few that persist. The lovely blue chicory, a rather late flowerer, often surprises us in those districts where it grows on the roadsides and edges of fields. The Compositae also give us most of the September garden flowers—Michaelmas daisies, dahlias, and chrysanthemums. These flowers—purples, golds, crimsons, yellows—are the signals warning us that October, and real autumn, is very near.

ANNIVERSARIES OF EVENTS, EPOCHS, AND RECORDS

2nd September 1666. The great fire of London broke out at a spot near London Bridge. Three hundred and ninety-six acres of the city were destroyed. With the flames went much dirt, squalor, and disease, as well as the old St. Paul's Cathedral and many other edifices. For three days 'horrible flakes of fire' mounted up the sky from the inferno of wooden houses, and 'if the sun peered forth it looked red like blood.' In the rebuilding brick and stone replaced wood—but whether the plan that was followed or that advocated by Sir Christopher Wren was the better, is still argued.

In 1752 this day was followed immediately by the 14th. The 3rd to 13th of September disappeared entirely: Thursday the 14th was next to Wednesday the 2nd. Thus the Julian or Old-Style calendar was converted to the New Style or Gregorian.

3rd September 1658. John Evelyn wrote: 'Died that arch rebell Oliver Cromwell, cal'd Protector.' There was a dreadful storm raging at the time, raised, the Royalists said, by the devil who had come to take Noll away within the terms of their compact. Or you can have it as does my old history book—'He never spared himself in the service of his country. When England was at her lowest he raised her to honour both at home and abroad.'

8th September 1402. On this night we have another magical storm. Owen Glendower raised a gale to attack the army of Henry IV. The wind was so powerful that it lifted Henry's lance which was flung against him; had he not been sleeping in his armour he must have been killed.

14th September 1852. Arthur Wellesley, Duke of Wellington, died. The English so dislike and disregard their soldiers that his memory should, perhaps, not be commemorated in our Almanac. But if we forget the soldier who started by studying and learning exactly what was the capability, power of endurance, and food requirements of his private soldier, who conducted a famous campaign in India, an even more famous one in the Peninsula, and was finally largely responsible for the overthrow of one of the greatest military geniuses in history—if we forget this and remember an astute but fearless and forthright man, who became a politician, granted Catholics their emancipation, endured a long period of unpopularity until in old age he became the idol of the people, then he may just creep in.

15th September 1784. Vincent Lunardi made the first aerial journey in England. He rose in his hydrogen balloon from the artillery ground at Moorfields, touched down at South Mimms, sailed up again, and finally landed at Standon near Ware. His passengers were a pigeon and a cat, both of which escaped, and a dog who remained faithful. His craft was well provisioned—the trip lasted two and a quarter hours—but unfortunately the food soon got mixed up with the sand ballast and was inedible.

15th September 1940. In the years following Lunardi's gas-lifted drift over Hertfordshire aircraft had developed to such an extent that on this day was fought an aerial battle so important as to mark a decisive phase in the most widespread war of history. The Luftwaffe made its greatest daylight attack on London. Like the battle of Waterloo it was on a Sunday, and like it the result was decisive. Britain, so nearly defeated in the sky, thenceforward maintained the upper hand.

18th September. At Lichfield and Uttoxeter the memory of Dr. Johnson is commemorated on this, the anniversary of his birth at Lichfield in 1709. His literary work, good though it was, is largely forgotten, and he remains a melancholy, unforgettable master of one-sided dialogue through the accident of having a genius, Boswell, as his biographer.

The Lichfield choirboys recite his last prayer as a wreath is laid on his statue; on the same day at Uttoxeter a sermon is preached in the market square telling the school children of the sad quarrel that young Johnson had with his father, and which unhappily remained unhealed.

Johnson died on 13th December—a month he hated—in 1784.

23rd September. On this day we may celebrate the arrival of the lawn-mower, for on it Mr. J. C. Loudon saw the new machine working successfully at the Zoological Society's gardens in Regent's Park. He wrote an enthusiastic account of it in his *Gardener's Magazine*, and before long his prophecy that it would be outstandingly successful was fulfilled. Until its use all lawns were scythed. The machine was made by J. Ferrabee of the Phoenix Foundery [*sic*], Stroud, and was priced at from seven to ten guineas.

23rd September 1844. Barry the Clown of Astley's Theatre sailed from Vauxhall Bridge to Westminster Bridge in a wash-tub drawn by four geese. So far as I know this still stands as a record, and as such we shall choose it for September.

27th September 1825. With the designer, George Stephenson, on the footplate of the locomotive, the first railway line, from Stockton to Darlington, was opened. The train carried six wagons loaded with coal and flour, and one with humans. A rider on horseback went in front, waving a flag. The incredulous crowd saw Stephenson signal him to one side, and, accelerating to fifteen miles per hour, leave the horse behind.

29th September 1613. The citizens of London assembled to witness and celebrate the entrance of the New River to the city. It brought the first good supply of water that London ever had, drawn from Hertfordshire and Middlesex. Boards and committees failed to make any progress with the scheme. Then a young goldsmith, later to become Sir Hugh Myddleton, tackled the job, and successfully overcame the formidable obstacles and not inconsiderable opposition.

THE POET

'It would seem,' wrote that arbiter of taste and exemplar of learning, the writer of a fourth leader in *The Times*, 'that poets have always grown exhausted as the summer wears, so little attention have they paid to

September.'   He claims in support the evidence of 'those invaluable allies the books of quotation.'   But I have found that, valuable though they are in rallying to help the compiler during the fine days of spring and summer, their support languishes in the colder and less pleasant months of the year.

The conclusions reached by *The Times* I must also dispute.   Fighting my battle unaided I have found much that not only relates to and names the month, but also a great deal referring to the end of summer, which, I take it, occurs during September.

For example, there is John Drinkwater's *Summer's End*:

> Go, green-man Summer, get you hence,
>   Your mistress Autumn bids you go;
> The larches of your innocence
>   Burn out; your virgins are the sloe.
>
> Your pools grow dark; your groves are rust;
>   Your withered stalks are rank with dew;
> Your poppies are a little dust;
>   Your martins have forsaken you.
>
> Beautiful garlands of decay,
>   Seal up your song and quench your light;
> No more at eve the ghost of day
>   Lingers with you to keep the night.
>
> The canker that your roses feared,
>   Itself is clay; and clay the rose;
> Your woodbine now is old-man's-beard—
>   You have no further lease of those.
>
> Lest memory were too great a cost,
>   Our joy of you with you shall set,
> And we will grieve our Summer lost,
>   And, even as we grieve, forget.

And these well-known lines of Keats describe the last days of September as he walked along the banks of the Itchen below Winchester a week before Michaelmas Day:

Where are the songs of Spring?   Ay, where are they?
Think not of them, thou hast thy music too,—
While barrèd clouds bloom the soft-dying day,
And touch the stubble-plains with rosy hue;
Then in a wailful choir the small gnats mourn
Among the river sallows, borne aloft
Or sinking as the light wind lives or dies;
And full-grown lambs loud bleat from hilly bourn;
Hedge-crickets sing; and now with treble soft
The redbreast whistles from a garden-croft;
And gathering swallows twitter in the skies.

The Times regretted that there was no poet of football to welcome its arrival during the month.   But a century or so ago Thomas Haynes Bayly wrote this punning doggerel on a lady's regrets at what was then *the* sporting event of the month:

Don't talk of September!—a lady
   Must think it of all months the worst!
The men are preparing already
   To take themselves off on the First:
I try to arrange a small party,
   The girls dance together—how tame!
I 'd get up *my* game of écarté,
   But *they* go to bring down *their* game.

There are several more verses, with the italicized puns getting progressively worse and worse.   Another September ingenuity is that of Sir John Davies, who ended a life full of incident by dying immediately after his appointment as Lord Chief Justice of England by James I:

E ach month has praise in some degree;
L et May to others seem to be
I n sense the sweetest season;
S eptember thou art best to me,
A nd best dost please my reason.

B ut neither for thy corn nor wine
E xtol I those mild days of thine,
T hough corn and wine might praise thee;
H eaven gives thee honour more divine,
A nd higher fortunes raise thee.

R enown'd art thou (sweet month) for this,
E mong thy days her birth-day is;
G race, plenty, peace and honour,
I n one fair hour with her were born;
N ow since they still her crown adorn,
A nd still attend upon her.

His biographer wrote: 'Whether Elizabeth bestowed any marks of her favour does not appear.'

There is Christina Rossetti's *September*:

My song is half a sigh
Because my green leaves die;
Sweet are my fruits, but all my leaves are dying;
And well may Autumn sigh,
And well may I
Who watch the sere leaves flying.

My leaves that fade and fall,
I note you one and all;
I call you, and the Autumn wind is calling,
Lamenting for your fall,
And for the pall
You spread on earth in falling.

And here 's a song of flowers to suit such hours:
A song of the last lilies, the last flowers,
Amid my withering bowers.

In the sunny garden bed
Lilies look so pale,
Lilies droop the head
In the shady grassy vale;
If all alike they pine
In shade and in shine,
If everywhere they grieve,
Where will lilies live?

And Wordsworth, as usual in sonnet form, has *The Spur of Winter—September 1815*:

While not a leaf seems faded; while the fields,
With ripening harvest prodigally fair,
In brightest sunshine bask; this nipping air,

Sent from some distant clime where Winter wields
His icy scimitar, a foretaste yields
Of bitter change, and bids the flowers beware;
And whispers to the silent birds, 'Prepare
Against the threatening foe your trustiest shields.'
For me, who under kindlier laws belong
To Nature's tuneful quire, this rustling dry
Through leaves yet green, and yon crystalline sky,
Announce a season potent to renew,
'Mid frost and snow, the instinctive joys of song,
And nobler cares than listless summer knew.

Surely, therefore, we claim that our poets have celebrated September with due regard, if only by singing as

When Grasshopper, chirping late,
Easing thus his merry heart,
Not from cares but over-joy
Tells that Summer 's out of date . . .

OCTOBER  LIBRA

OCTOBER, with thirty-one days, is the tenth month. It was originally the eighth, hence *octo*.

Anglo-Saxons named it the month of the full moon in which winter begins, Winterfylleth as well as Wynmonath, the month when wine—and one supposes cider and perry—were made.

We might call it bonfire month, for in gardens and towns there is much sweeping up and burning of summer's fallen remains. The scent of the month is in their smoke. We are forcibly reminded that it is now time to adapt ourselves and make ready for winter with its colds and overcoats.

There is one event that should be recalled, though it is not an English anniversary. But its consequences to us have been considerable. On the night of Friday, 12th October 1492, Christopher Columbus sighted a moonlit coast-line; America was officially discovered.

It is the month of apple-harvest, the one fruit that we can grow to greater perfection than any other country. Pears, too, are picked.

THE WEATHER

October as often as not is the wettest month in the year. The difference between its average temperature and hours of sunshine, and the corresponding figures for September, is nearly always greater than in any other month; the sun now quite loses the mastery and surrenders to the moon without more ado.

161

Yet unseasonable echoes of summer are not unusual; by tradition we are liable to have a 'little summer' about the 18th, St. Luke's Day. We have, indeed, had October temperatures well over 80° F. in London. As against this 7° F. of frost have been recorded on the ground. The normal for the month is just under 50° F.

There have been heavy October fogs.

Weather sayings relate October abundance—from beechmast, fatness in badgers, to fogs—with severe weather in the coming winter.

THE HEAVENS

In the last week of the month the sun declines from Libra into the sign of Scorpio, the Scorpion.

In October, under the original Summer Time Act of 1925, we should put our clocks back one hour to ordinary time, but in the last years the period of Summer Time has been varied.

The first full moon after the equinoctial moon is famed as the hunter's moon.

FEASTS, FAIRS, AND FESTIVALS

3rd October.

Nottingham still holds its goose fair on this day. Geese were once the chief product of the district.

10th October.   Michaelmas Day, Old Style.

The Monday after this day is Pack Monday, or St. Michael's Fair, at Sherborne. It is ushered in by the youth of the district parading the village making as much noise as is possible with bugles, trays, and similar instruments. It is said that this ceremony commemorates the celebration in the fifteenth century by workmen who had completed building a particularly tricky bit of Sherborne Abbey.

12th October.

At Stratford-on-Avon the annual mop fair opens. Mops are relics of the old hiring fairs at which the workers, standing in rows, each carrying the insignia or implement of his calling, were engaged by the employers for a year. This usually ran from Michaelmas to Michaelmas, and so the fairs were mostly held just before old Michaelmas Day, which was 10th October.

Stratford Mop still draws great crowds.

13th October.   Translation of St. Edward the Confessor.

This Norman king of the Anglo-Saxons died in 1066, having achieved a 'reputation for superior sanctity,' and the rebuilding of Westminster Abbey. But he was not much good as a king.   He had a blunt sword of state, Curtana, emblematical of mercy.   Pope Alexander III canonized him in 1163.

17th October.   St. Ethelreda.

Ethelreda was daughter of Annas, King of the East Angles, and was born at Ixning in Suffolk.   Though twice forced by her family to marry she kept her vow to remain a nun, and claimed to be twice a widow, and always a virgin.   She died in 679, abbess of a convent that she had founded in Ely.

Her name became corrupted to St. Audrey, and under this name her festival was celebrated at Ely by a fair.   Cheap and showy laces and clothes were much in evidence—hence the word 'tawdry.'

18th October.   St. Luke.   Evangelist.

Few facts are known about this saint, so we may regard him through traditional eyes as the writer of the gospel and collaborator in the authorship of the Acts of the Apostles, a physician and painter who made a portrait of the Virgin.

He has therefore become patron saint of physicians and artists.   His symbol is an ox, representing sacrifice, since he wrote pre-eminently of the sacrifice of Christ.

In the times when Charlton was a village near London the inhabitants held a horn fair on this day, parading with horns on their heads.   This is thought to have been connected with St. Luke's ox.

19th October.   St. Crispin and St. Crispinian.

These two early martyrs are traditionally patrons of 'the art, mystery, calling, or occupation of shoemaking.'

The day is best remembered from the speech delivered before Agincourt by Shakespeare's Henry V. In this bloody battle nine thousand English archers defeated sixty thousand Frenchmen, killing eleven thousand of them. The effort exhausted the English army, and the king had to return to England to rebuild it.

21st October. Trafalgar Day.

On this day is celebrated the spirit in which Lord Nelson lived, fought, and died. Loved by the people, who looked upon him as their only deliverer from Napoleon (Devonians believed him to be a reincarnation of Drake), grief at his death overshadowed joy at his victory. Wreaths are laid at the foot of his monument in Trafalgar Square; they include an anchor from the descendants of the officers who fought with him and evergreens from the modern namesakes of his own ships. At Portsmouth his Trafalgar signal is flown and a ceremony held on his flagship *Victory.*

28th October. St. Simon and St. Jude. Apostles and Martyrs.

Historically these are shadowy figures. One legend says that Simon visited and was martyred in Britain. His symbols are a saw and fish—for traditionally he was a fishmonger. St. Jude was a carpenter and holds a carpenter's square in one hand. He often bears a staff or club.

Once upon a time a legend similar to that of St. Swithin belonged to their day.

31st October. All Hallows Even or Hallowe'en.

This day was anciently one of the great fire festivals of the northern hemisphere, the eve of the beginning of winter on the first day of November, which was in pagan times also a day dedicated to the cult of the dead. The Church made it the vigil of All Saints' Day.

The bonfires were burned to strengthen the sun, the ashes afterwards being scattered on the land to bring fertility. In some places, particularly the north, the fires were lit and local ceremonies and superstitions practiced until the last century. But now the pagan customs have almost universally been transferred to dishonour poor old Guy Fawkes!

Hallowe'en games were played in the evening. One of them was diving for apples. Suspended or floated, they had to be grasped in the teeth while both hands were tied behind the back.

It was a night for nut-eating; they were also used for divination. Marked with the names of pairs of lovers they were put in the edge of the fire. If they sizzled and spat then their namesakes would do likewise; a pair jumping apart indicated incompatibility, while those lying peacefully together gave promise of quiet and happiness.

It is generally agreed that ghosts and goblins are still abroad on this night.

THE SPORTSMAN

October is devoted to the pheasant, which, except for Sundays and Christmas Day, can be killed from the 1st of the month onwards.

The bird is not native to our shore; *Phasianus colchicus*, mentioned as being here in 1059, has crossed with *P. torquatus* from China introduced two centuries or more ago. One or two other strains have been added, and our modern pheasant is, therefore, a mongrel. Because of this, and because of the artificial rearing and protection, some writers call it a semi-domesticated creature.

Rearing of pheasants on a large scale for modern pheasant shooting did not become fashionable until the breech-loading gun came into general use in the latter part of the nineteenth century. Carefully organized mass slaughtering of tame birds was at its most popular during the early years of the twentieth century. Financial worries have, fortunately, now once again made pheasant shooting rather more of a sport.

But we hope that the bird will never disappear. Apart from its sporting admirers there can be few who will not agree with the Rev. Sydney Smith's opinion that 'if there be one pure and elevated pleasure in the world it is a roast pheasant. Barn-door fowls for Dissenters, but for we Churchmen, the thirty-nine times articled clerk, the pheasant, the pheasant.'

For the rest, Badminton comes in with the month, stalking of stags ends in the middle, and salmon fishing with rods goes out at the end of it.

Badminton is an organized form of the ancient amusement of battledore and shuttlecock. It seems to have been developed by the English community in India, for rules for its conduct were drawn up at Karachi in 1877. It proved an ideal game for large country house-parties in late Victorian and

Edwardian days, and now becomes an energetic relaxation for many in the winter evenings when lawn tennis is no longer possible.

Flat racing has some of its last important events, including the Cambridgeshire and Cesarewitch Stakes, both run at Newmarket.

THE NATURALIST

Autumn's processes are very subtle and complex. They produce remarkable effects—the brilliant colouring of leaves and fruit and the miracle of hibernation, which may be almost complete suspension of life. One fundamental difference between this season and spring lies in there being no increase in external structure, nor reproduction. The changes—ripening of fruit, fall of leaf, and hibernation—are internal and, but for a flash of colour, invisible. Perhaps that is why so much attention is given to charting the progress of spring and summer, of which there is abundant superficial evidence, and little to autumn when practically all is hidden—indeed, much life goes out of its way to hide—and so rather mysterious.

Death, a quite universal and unescapable cause of change and, therefore, somewhat displeasing, also plays a great part in autumn. The first frosts kill a myriad insects and other small creatures. Yet they will have taken 'all reasonable and necessary steps' to perpetuate their race in accordance with their usual practice. It is just too bad if man sweeps up the eggs into a bonfire.

The most spectacular sign of these changes is the colouring and then falling leaves of trees and shrubs. The first of these stages, for some reason known as 'the autumn tints,' reaches its gayest during October. At the joint of each leaf-stalk where it joins the twig a thin layer is formed between the two. The leaf is gradually cut out of the circulatory system of the tree. Its chemical composition undergoes great changes, and this results in bright colours replacing the former green. Finally it becomes so loosely attached to the twig that it falls at a slight touch. On the ground, woven into a carpet of other leaves, it gradually decays and returns some of the energy that has been employed in its creation back to the earth. The scar on the twig has been healed against the entry of fungus or other enemy.

This, of course, happens each year with deciduous trees. Evergreens, such as rhododendrons and conifers, undergo the same cycle, but the life of each leaf is several years.

Changes also occur within the ripening fruit. From our and some birds' and animals' point of view, the development of sugars in some kinds which makes them palatable is not the least important. It also serves what to us is a secondary end—the distribution of the seeds by those who consume the surrounding pulpy mass.

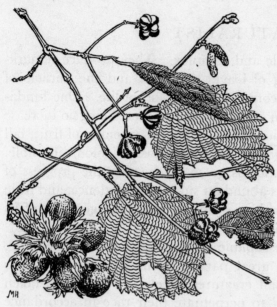

Spindle-berries and Hazel-nuts

A good number of late-summer plants still flower, particularly annual weeds of cultivated ground. A blaze of dahlias and chrysanthemums remains in the garden until it is blackened by frost. Some of our introduced conifers, such as the cedars, will be opening their catkin-like male flowers and scattering pollen during this month. The arbutus or strawberry-tree, which is believed to have survived as a native of these islands in Ireland during an age when much else perished, bears panicles of little white or pinkish urn-like flowers which turn into 'strawberries.'

But most vegetable vigour is seen in the great army of fungi which throw up their spore-bearing devices—toadstools, shaggy-caps, puff-balls, bracket fungi, and moulds and mildews—in great abundance during late autumn. It is a numerous and powerful army. In this country it includes some seven thousand species against fifteen hundred of ordinary seed-bearing plants.

Once again migration on a big scale excites bird watchers. Not only do we greet more winter visitors, but see many birds of passage. It is not, perhaps, realized how many of our common and resident kinds are also migrants.

T. A. Coward [1] writes of these October movements seen near the lighthouse on The Spurn in Yorkshire: '. . . the watcher can never guess what he may see any morning, nor how many thousands have drifted by during the night unseen, unheard. The grey geese, in small skeins, passed at sea; ducks of many kinds floated by, or took flights close to the water; the first of the Brent geese was spotted. . . . On dark or foggy nights the southward flight of many individuals is checked by dazzling rays from the lighthouse . . . before me is one night's report when knots, redwings, fieldfares, blackbirds, starlings, lapwings, golden plovers, a rail, and a goldcrest struck in a fog.'

Pink-footed Goose

Swallows, house- and sand-martins, as well as the last of the wheatear, leave us early in the month. Fieldfare, redwing, brambling, and wigeon are the principal arrivals—with, of course, geese as the great excitement. It is a month when we may glimpse passing rarities; even osprey have been reported in Surrey. It is also a time when the little birds are flocking. Blackbirds and robins take up their territory.

For many animals it is the month when hibernation begins. In its varying degrees from partial to almost complete lifelessness it is a form of wintering adopted by creatures ranging from butterflies to badgers. Sometimes insect hibernators will be found in colonies—peacock butterflies and queen wasps, or ladybirds, perhaps in some warm space between boarding; at others they will hide singly in cracks between all kinds of odd material.

Bats also hibernate, hanging head downwards, in buildings, caves, or hollow trees; sometimes they too are found singly in crevices. Dormice roll

[1] *Bird Haunts and Nature Memories.*

up in nests, underground or beneath roots and shrubs, with a good supply of food in case warm spells wake them up. The adder joins with one or two friends in sharing a hollow among heather or dry grass. Grass snakes collect together in large numbers beneath old roots, under piles of brushwood, or in dry holes. Blindworms burrow with their heads into loose dry soil, or similar material; this they do very early in autumn. Lizards also dig themselves in, often quite deeply, joining together in small colonies. Frogs hibernate in many odd places—holes, under piles of leaves, hayricks, and so on. Toads become comatose only, and prefer a dry hole, well away from water. Newts go underground; numbers are often found twined together in a mass.

One other October occurrence is the rut, or mating season of deer. The stags are savage, and will attack people and dogs. They fight for possession of the hinds. With red deer the season usually starts in September and lasts through October; fallow deer have a shorter period starting rather later. It is the only time when male deer make any noise. This, the 'belling' of red deer, has been described by E. W. Hendy: [1]

'Heard at night, especially in stormy weather, . . . belling is a weird and disquieting sound. While the wind sobs and whimpers through woods already thinning from leaves, and clouds scurry fearfully across a murky sky, there comes fitfully out of the distant gloom a deep-pitched booming; its *timbre* is that of a bull's bellow; but in it is not anger alone, but pain and unrest, the moan of insatiate ocean on a rock-bound coast, the soughing of a gale through bare and desolate boles.'

ANNIVERSARIES OF EVENTS, EPOCHS, AND RECORDS

1st October 1795. Robert Bakewell died near Loughborough, where he was born in 1725. His is a name shouldered out of history books by insignificant politicians, but his value to the country, and indeed, the world, is great—a pioneer in agriculture who laid down the basis for breeding livestock to type and requirements. He set out to prove his belief that 'you can get beasts to weigh *where* you want them to weigh,' by producing breeds that conformed to standards—his Dishley and Leicestershire long-horn cattle, Leicestershire sheep, and a once famous race of black horses. He was one of the first to

[1] *Wild Exmoor through the Year.*

170

study the proper feeding and keeping of stock, and also made successful experiments in irrigating fields. His income was considerable, but scarcely covered the costs of his experiments, and he died a poor man.

1st October 1861. This was the publication day for the first volume of *Beeton's Book of Household Management*, edited by Mrs. Isabella Beeton—better known simply as 'Mrs. Beeton.' The work had previously been well received by the public when issued in serial parts.

2nd October 1858. The clock Big Ben on the Houses of Parliament was started.

5th October 1730. To the order of Queen Caroline, and under the direction of Charles Withers, Esq. and Mr. Jephson, the construction of the Serpentine was begun in Hyde Park.

8th October 1754. Henry Fielding, novelist and justice for Middlesex, died in Lisbon—cheerful, courageous, and still writing to the last. He was born of good family in Somersetshire on 22nd April 1707. After what at first appeared to be a misspent youth he became a writer of burlesques (his tilts at the government resulted in the institution of the censorship of plays), and then of his great novels with plots that flow on like some river on the banks of which are seen, as we pass, a continual series of vistas displaying the life of the day —indeed, often of human nature itself, unadorned and behaving slightly comically and without self-consciousness. His apparently wasted youth had in reality given him a profound knowledge of the world. This was also put to good use in his valuable service as a magistrate. In an age when most literature is written in a spirit of self-conscious gloom, we commemorate him as the founder of the English comic novel, showing the people of the country as they are.

10th October. To-day we celebrate the introduction of two amenities that the mechanical age has brought about.

First, in 1881 the Savoy theatre opened in London with Gilbert and Sullivan's *Patience*. This was a singular event for two reasons: it was the first theatre in England to be lit by electric light (there were no 'mains' in those days—steam-engines on a neighbouring waste land drove the dynamos), and secondly, because a new system of booking seats was introduced from France. It had the novel name of a *queue*.

Then in 1899 the first London motor-bus service began. It ran between Kennington and Victoria, by way of Westminster. The pioneer passengers suffered much discomfort and from fumes; horse-bus drivers laughed at this oily vehicle, which would soon disappear from the streets, leaving the eternal horse unmolested and supreme.

14th October 1066. Duke William of Normandy defeated Harold II, King of the English. The battle was fought at Senlac near Hastings. William played a most un-British trick on us; his forces having simulated defeat Harold's men careered after them in victorious disorder. The Normans launched a savage counter-attack and won the day. It is true that the English were also suffering from having seen an omen—Halley's comet having made an appearance.
The battle is so well known that we are in honour bound to make it an epoch.

15th October 1839. The young Queen Victoria summoned Albert, Duke of Saxe-Coburg-Gotha, to her room, and abruptly proposed marriage to him. It was, she said, 'a nervous thing to do,' but as for proposing to the Queen of England, 'he would never have presumed to take such a liberty.'

18th October 1826. The draw for the last English state lottery was held. A number of tickets remained unsold. The state lost an income of £250,000 a year, and the lottery-keepers, who rented expensive offices in all the principal cities, a good job.

19th October. This day is dedicated to the railway.

On it in 1839 George Bradshaw published his first railway guide. The project was opposed by the railway companies, who took the view that it would make the punctual departure of their trains an obligation.

More recently, in 1946, Alexander Marshall, a Portsmouth crane-driver, succeeded in pulling three goods wagons weighing nineteen tons a distance of fifty feet with his teeth. This will suffice as our October record.

23rd October 1915. No English almanac would be complete without a reference to one of England's most lasting heroes, Dr. W. G. Grace, who died on this day in 1915. He was born near Bristol on 18th July 1848, and later practised there as a doctor for some twenty years. He became the greatest national figure in the game of cricket, a player of unequalled skill. During his playing career of no less than forty-three years he made 126 centuries, scored 54,896 runs, and took 2,876 wickets.

25th October 1400. We must claim as English at heart Geoffrey Chaucer, who died on this day—soldier, courtier, diplomat, traveller, and, above all, poet. He was aged about sixty. Unfortunately he wrote in a language that is now less understandable to most of us than the commoner foreign languages, but through translations we are able to see his power as a story-teller, and his wide knowledge of men and the world of fourteenth-century England.

THE POET

'Bright October was come, the misty-bright October, . . .' wrote Clough, and with it undoubtedly comes autumn, whose arrival is a great theme for our poets.

Two rural authors associate its glories with the pig. Bloomfield wrote:

> Again, the year's decline, midst storm and floods,
> The thundering chase, the yellow fading woods,
> Invite my song; that fain would boldly tell
> Of upland coverts, and the echoing dell,
> By turns resounding loud, at eve and morn
> The swineherd's halloo, or the huntsman's horn.

> No more the fields with scatter'd grain supply
> The restless wandering tenants of the sty;
> From oak to oak they run with eager haste,
> And wrangling share the first delicious taste
> Of fallen acorns; yet but thinly found
> Till the strong gale has shook them to the ground.
> It comes; and roaring woods obedient wave:
> Their home well pleas'd the joint adventurers leave:
> The trudging sow leads forth her numerous young,
> Playful, and white, and clean, the briars among.

And a later poet—or perhaps he should be called rhymester—Will Carleton, is even more to the point:

> 'Tis in the thriftful Autumn days,
>   When earth is overdone
> And forest trees have caught the blaze
>   Thrown at them by the sun. . . .
>
> And in his barrel-coffin rests
>   The porker, doomed to die,
> Or, still the recent cruel sport
>   Of knife-engendered pangs,
> His blushing corpse, with lessened port,
>   Upon the gallows hangs;
> 'Tis then good prosperous folk display
>   A reverential cheer,
> And thank their Maker one whole day
>   For all the rest of the year.

At the beginning of the eighteenth century Thomas Brerewood welcomed autumn in a different manner:

> Though the seasons must alter, ah! yet let me find
>   What all must confess to be rare,
> A female still cheerful, and faithful and kind,
>   The blessings of autumn to share.
>   .   .   .   .   .   .
> When the vapours that rise from the earth in the morn
>   Seem to hang on its surface like smoke,
> Till dispers'd by the sun that gilds over the corn,
>   Within doors let us prattle and joke. . . .

While in Elizabethan days we have a vivid, hard picture in Nashe's lines:

> Autumn hath all the summer's fruitful treasure,
> Gone is our sport, fled is poor Corydon's pleasure.
> Short days, sharp days, long nights come on apace;
> Ah, who shall hide us from the winter's face?
> Cold doth increase, the sickness will not cease,
> And here we lie, God knows, with little ease;
> From winter, plague, and pestilence, good Lord, deliver us!

Of the month itself we have *The First Week in October* by that delightful and precise miniaturist, the clergyman who was the great Lord Tennyson's brother, and who took the name of Turner:

> Once on an Autumn day as I reposed
> Beneath a moon-beam, pallid yet not dull,
> The branch above my head dipt itself full
> Of that white sunshine momently, and closed;
> While ever and anon, the ashen keys
> Dropt down beside the tarnish'd hollyhocks,
> The scarlet crane's-bill, and the faded stocks—
> Flung from the shuffling leafage by the breeze.
> How wistfully I mark'd the year's decay,
> Forecasting all the dreary wind and rain;
> 'Twas the last week the swallow would remain—
> How jealously I watched his circling play!
> A few brief hours, and he would dart away,
> No more to turn upon himself again.

The robin's song is part of October.   Alice Meynell wrote of it—how, in a weary month, it sings the most joyous of all bird songs.

And Richard Church:

> One chill October morning
> When day broke white and wan,
> I heard a robin chitter.
> The cheery little man!
>
> 'Cheep!   Cheep!
> What shall I do with it?
> Cheep!   Cheep!
> Whatever shall I do with it?
> Cheep!   Chirrup!   Cheep!
> There 's nothing to be done
> With my old red waistcoat now I 've a new one.'
>
> Beech trees were beacons burning
> Above the swaying mist,
> Chestnut pods were falling
> And their brown nestlings lost.

The elms, still proud with summer,
Yet in their windward tops
Hung the pale signs of ruin,
Like fever-stricken ships.

And to this world of wreckage
Lit by a ghostly sun,
The robin piped his worry
In wistful voice and thin.

'Cheep!   Cheep!
What shall I do with it?
Cheep!   Cheep!
Whatever shall I do with it?
Cheep!   Chirrup!   Cheep!
Oh, there's nothing to be done
With my old red waistcoat now I've a new one.'

But let us be under no illusion.   October gives us days which make us realize that winter is near and inescapable.   So we see it in Robert Bridges's *North Wind in October*:

In the golden glade the chestnuts are fallen all;
From the sered boughs of the oak the acorns fall:
The beech scatters her ruddy fire;
The lime hath stripped to the cold,
And standeth naked above her yellow attire:
The larch thinneth her spire
To lay the ways of the wood with cloth of gold.

Out of the golden-green and white
Of the brake the fir-trees stand upright
In the forest of flame, and wave aloft
To the blue of heaven their blue-green tuftings soft.

But swiftly in shuddering gloom the splendours fail,
As the harrying North-wind beareth
A cloud of skirmishing hail
The grievèd woodland to smite:
In a hurricane through the trees he teareth,

Raking the boughs and the leaves rending
And whistleth to the descending
Blows of his icy flail.
Gold and snow he mixeth in spite,
And whirleth afar; as away on his winnowing flight
He passeth, and all again for awhile is bright.

NOVEMBER  SCORPIO

NOVEMBER, with thirty days, is our eleventh month. In the first Roman calendar it was the ninth, hence *novem*.

The Anglo-Saxons are supposed to have called it Windmonath, the windy month. Perhaps our present still and foggy days had not then arrived. They also named it Blodmonath, or blood month. This has been explained as due to the practice of slaughtering of cattle for salting-down or drying for winter use. Or, according to others, because of ancient and no doubt sombre sacrificial rites celebrated at this season.

We now see passing us in trucks or piled by the roadside ready for collections the grimy-white roots of sugar-beet, that most recent of crops that has become almost universally grown in the last two decades. When lifting starts we know that we are fast on the move to winter.

All that can now be said of the month as it passes gloomily by is summed up in the rhyme of Thomas Hood:

> No warmth, no cheerfulness, no healthful ease,
> No comfortable feel in any member—
> No shade, no shine, no butterflies, no bees,
> No fruits, no flowers, no leaves, no birds—
> November!

THE WEATHER

Not even the iconoclasm of scientific meteorology has disturbed the traditional—even international—reputation of our Novembers. Statistics prove what we have known for centuries, that it is a misty, gloomy, and often foggy

month. This is because there is usually little wind to move the airs that flow over us in our moist, island position. The rainfall is usually about the third heaviest of any month in the year.

The normal temperature for the month is between 43° F. and 44° F.

There are, however, exceptions to prove our rules. There is often an unseasonable warm spell. Legend relates it to Martinmas, the 11th, and calls it St. Martin's little summer; Buchan, however, disagrees as he gives his final cold spell to the days beginning with the 6th and ending on the 13th. Some authorities say that the fine days most usually arrive around All Saints' Day—the 1st.

Another exception to our breathless November gloom was in 1703. Then on the 27th the 'great storm in England' reached its height. For several days a west wind had been blowing stronger and stronger until it achieved an awful power. Darkness fell early. The gale made a noise 'hoarse and dreadful, like thunder, which carried terror to every ear.'

Damage done in London alone amounted to £2,000,000. In Gloucestershire 15,000 sheep were lost. The Eddystone lighthouse, with its designer, Winstanley, was swept away. Fortunately the fleet was well out at sea, and rode the storm with little harm.

Few weather sayings belong to the month; our old prophets were presumably befogged.

THE HEAVENS

On about the 24th the sun passes from Scorpio into Sagittarius, the Archer.

FEASTS, FAIRS, AND FESTIVALS

1st November. All Saints' Day. All Souls' Eve.

The Church on this day honours all those saints who do not qualify for a special day of their own, and who, in heaven, from their labours rest. It is also called All Hallows and even All Hollands.

In folklore and tradition, however, it is as the eve of the day on which souls in purgatory are remembered that the 1st of November is important.

On it 'souling,' or the begging of alms by the poor to assist the souls of their dead relatives, took place. This custom developed many forms. Souling by children—singing for a soul-cake—possibly still survives, though pence or sweets may now be the reward.

More interesting are the souling plays, which retained relics, sometimes a little sinister, of the old pagan rites. The plot was simple in outline—some sort of a hero overcame and eventually killed his adversary. The detail varied. It might be St. George and the dragon. In another version the victim was 'a black Morocca dog,' and in others a human was slain. When, as in some localities, Hob the Horse took a part, the ceremony was called hodening. A horse's head was obtained from a knacker's yard, and so arranged that by means of strings the lifeless jaws could be snapped together.

Souling and hodening continued into the last century in some country districts. We have quite recent accounts of the bands of players, usually farm labourers, taking their plays to the farms and large country houses.

2nd November. All Souls Day.

The Church can have had little difficulty in diverting the attention of the pagans from their practice of honouring the dead to the Christian festival in which they sought alleviation from the torments of the souls of their friends and relatives in purgatory. For, on the 1st of November 993 Odilo, abbot of Clugny, heard at first hand such a story as to convince the most hardened of the urgent need to pray for tortured souls. It was told to him by a pilgrim who, on returning from the Holy Land, was shipwrecked on a rocky island. There he met a hermit who showed him, among the cliffs, an opening into the infernal regions. From its depths huge flames curled into the sky; the terrible groans of the tormented were clearly audible. Odilo at once set aside the next day as one of intercession for the souls dwelling in this inferno.

In medieval times men in black went about the towns ringing mournful bells, calling for prayers in aid of those in purgatory.

5th November. Guy Fawkes's Day.

> Please to remember
> The fifth of November,
> With gunpowder treason and plot . . .

So we come to the one fire festival that still exists. Somehow the flames that burnt atavistically on Hallowe'en have got themselves transferred as a memorial to Guy Fawkes, who on this night in 1605 was discovered in his attempt to blow up the Houses of Parliament. His effigy is burnt—or anyhow, a big enough fire is made to burn it—and black-faced boys parade demanding a penny for the guy. Above all, fireworks are let off. Those ignited by the genteel are floriferous, coloured, sparkling, and ascend to compete with the stars; those fused by the less genteel merely go bang, very loudly. The great art of pyrotechny by night belongs to midsummer, to royal and famous occasions. But of late it has become more and more attached to Guy Fawkes's night.

The plot is remembered in other ways. There are still remains of bonfire societies with their 'No Popery' banners. Yeomen of the Guard still search the Houses. A service of thanks at its discovery was not removed from the Prayer Book until 1859.

At Edenbridge in Kent there is a torchlight procession of the school children, followed by tableaux. It moves slowly to the music of bands through the village to the bonfire field. People from far away come to see it. Guy Fawkes plays but a small part in the ceremony.

At Rye a boat is burned. It is carried at the head of a procession to a water meadow called the Town Salts, where it is ceremoniously set alight.

At Lewes, too, the bonfires are built and burned with organized pomp and ceremony.

9th November.   The Lord Mayor's Show.

Many centuries have enshrined their traditions in Lord Mayor of London's Show. On 8th November he has been elected, with the king's assent, and since the sixteenth century (and probably earlier) has on the next day taken part in this pageant. Until the beginning of the eighteenth century he rode on horseback, but subsequently his heavy carriage was used. A century ago part of the journey, from Blackfriars Bridge to Westminster, where he was sworn-in, was made by river, and the Lord Mayor's barge master in his state dress followed by the bargemen in their gay colours made a fine feature in the procession.

11th November. *St. Martin or Martinmas.*

St. Martin started life as a soldier, and by all accounts was a gallant and genial man. He divided his cloak with a beggar, and subsequently saw a vision which caused him to retire from the army and take to the Church. He was so excellent at working miracles that by popular wish he was made Bishop of Tours.

He is the patron of France. Perhaps because Martinmas coincides with the old Roman Bacchanalia, and also the period at which beef and pigs had to be killed so that they might be preserved through the long winter, this saint has become associated with wine and food. He is the patron of reformed drunkards.

On this day, too, was signed an armistice between the contending forces in the Great War in 1918. Flanders poppies, made by disabled soldiers, are worn to recall those who were killed in the fighting.

'Wroth Silver'—a token sum in dues—is paid by certain parishes near Dunchurch to the Duke of Buccleuch. By so doing they retain an ancient right to drive cattle across his land.

13th November.

'Bull-running' at Stamford was once an occasion of wide fame. Briefly, bulls were let loose in the streets of the town, and pursued by men armed with clubs, and by dogs, and treated with every form of brutality.

20th November. *St. Edmund.* *King of East Anglia and Martyr.*

When his kingdom was invaded by the Danes Hingwar and Hubba, Edmund attacked them, but was defeated and captured. Freedom was offered to him if he would rule under the Danes, but this he proudly refused to do. Thereupon he was martyred and his body thrown into a thicket. His followers went to find the corpse. Hearing a voice they traced it to its source, and there found Edmund's detached head. It was guarded by a wolf which suffered the searchers to approach so that they might mark the spot. On their return later the head now had the body attached, a purple line marking the join.

That was in 870. Edmund became a popular hero. Much folklore—some a transference to him of pagan legend—gathered round his name. He was canonized in 1222. A church was built on this spot where his head was so miraculously found, and around it grew the town that became known as Bury St. Edmunds.

22nd November. St. Cecilia. Virgin and Martyr.

Cecilia lived in the days of the pagan Emperor of Rome, Alexander Severus. She was both beautiful and blind. While quite young, together with her family, she had embraced Christianity, and taken a vow to remain virginal.

Her skill as a musician was remarkable, and one day, Timotheus, an angel, hearing her play on the organ (which she had invented) came down and paid the first of many visits. In the meantime her parents had arranged her marriage with an eligible but pagan young Roman named Valerian.

Cecilia decided to tell him of her vows and visitations. Valerian was immediately converted to Christianity, and Timotheus promised them both the crown of martyrdom.

Cecilia was roasted in her bath. She died 'singing to God in her heart.'

She is patron of the blind, but, above all, of music. Odes by Dryden and Pope and music by Blow, Purcell, and Handel, as well as by more recent composers, honour the last. Lately the custom of celebrating the day with music, sometimes with the old pieces, and at others with new works specially composed, has most happily been revived.

23rd November. St. Clement. Bishop and Martyr.

Clement lived during the first century after Christ. As a theological writer he is still considered important, but little is known of him historically.

We will therefore assume that tradition is true and that he was born a tanner, and is patron of tanners. Other authors claim him as patron of blacksmiths in addition.

He somehow became connected with a custom of begging drink—with which to get merry—on this day. It is said to be of Danish origin. As a result his emblem is a pot.

At one time children used to be decked up in finery and led in procession on St. Clement's Day.

25th November. St. Catherine. Virgin and Martyr.

Historically, we are told, nothing is known of this famous saint, whose miraculous escape from death in the jaws of a savage machine has given the name to that most ingenious and delightful firework, the Catherine wheel.

Her legend, as we must call it, is this. She came of a distinguished Alexandrian family in the fourth century, when Maximin II was Emperor of Rome. Converted to Christianity, her explanation and defence of its doctrines was so eloquent that her opponents were routed. Annoyed, the pagan emperor called all his wisest men together so that they might confute her. This they failed to do, and were accordingly burnt.

Catherine, in spite of her victory, was to be destroyed by a fiendish device of spiked wheels. This was, however, struck by lightning just as they started to turn, her bonds were severed, and she was saved.

Unconvinced by this miracle the emperor had her carried outside the walls of the city and slain by more normal methods. Her body was then picked up by angels, carried across the Red Sea, and placed on Mount Sinai.

This saint has become the patron of girls.

30th November. St. Andrew. Apostle and Martyr.

Andrew of Bethsaida in Galilee was brother to Simon Peter. He was a fisherman, and once a disciple of John the Baptist. He was called from his nets by Christ to be a fisher of men.

Traditionally his later ministry was in Scythia, Greece, and Thrace. He was martyred on an X-shaped cross at Patrae in Achaea (Greece). This is his emblem.

He is patron of Scotland because, it is said, his body was brought to where St. Andrews now stands. There are those who claim that this is a mistake, and that the real patron is not Andrew, but a monk named Rule or Regulus, who, coming to Scotland from the place of Andrew's death—Patrae—was later confused with the apostle.

There is little other tradition connected with this day, though at Easling in Kent it was once the occasion for a squirrel-hunting festival.

THE SPORTSMAN

November's calendar gives pride of place to the horse. Steeplechasing comes into its own, and flat racing goes out. Cubbing ends and hunting of the fox begins. On Exmoor hunting of red deer begins with the hind as quarry.

Racing on the flat goes out in the week that includes 22nd November. Lingfield Park and Manchester meetings end the season—the Manchester November Handicap, run traditionally in gloom, is the last big race of the year.

Hunting the fox is now the most popular form of hunting on horseback. At the time when Gawain was entertained by three days' hunting on the estate of the Green Knight, Sir Bercilak de Hautdesert, the fox came third. Stag and boar took precedence. Even in the latter part of the eighteenth century —when men like Peter Beckford pursued foxes—many considered the hare a superior quarry. But now, the field increased by great numbers of women, who during the present century have so numerously taken to equitation, there is no doubt about the overwhelming popularity of the fox hunt.

Hunting of the red deer begins on Exmoor during November with hinds as quarry. In the north stalking of hinds also begins in the middle of the month.

Perhaps a word should be said about golf in St. Andrew's month, for he must surely be its patron saint. The existence of the St. Andrews Club, which now controls the destiny of the game, is recorded in a document of 14th May 1754. It was probably not the first club to be formed, and certainly not the first to be granted regality. Blackheath claims to be senior. But in 1834 William IV bestowed its present prefix, both Royal and Ancient. It undoubtedly succeeds, however, in its claim to be the first club to lay out a special course for women in 1867. England followed at Westward Ho! in 1873.

Golfing events are so numerous and widely spread over the year—only record-breaking bad weather halts them—that the almanacker trying to grasp only a few salient features of the sporting year must miss many famous golfing occasions, and endeavour to repair his omissions this month. Let us then pay tribute to this most ancient game under whose rules kings and artisans, the old and new worlds, have so often in its long history been made equals.

THE NATURALIST

The first frosts bring a final blaze of colour to our trees; chrysanthemum growers win honour and glory for their achievements; robins sing cheerfully, and on sunny mornings so do thrushes—though we must wait until the darkest days are over before we hear their full song.　A few herbs go on flowering—
shepherd's purse, groundsel, chickweed, knotgrass.　Gorse always has a few golden blossoms.　But nothing is growing except the fungi.　Toadstools and puffballs still spring up among the fallen leaves and in grass, while fleshy brackets grow bigger and bigger on ancient trees and rotting stumps.

A few heavy storms and we are left in no doubt that the edge of winter has been reached; the mantle of green and coloured foliage has disappeared.　We are left with the naked curves of the earth over which is erected a bare network of branching trees and shrubs.

Woodland Toadstools

We see again the browns, reds, and greys of soil as the plough, with its black and white attendants, rooks and gulls, turns it over.

As the leaves fall bird watching in woodlands and gardens becomes still easier, though there is now little song to help in identification.　Migration has slowed down again, but there are further arrivals, such as goldcrests from the north and invasions of wood-pigeons from the Continent.　The golden-eye and harriers may be seen as birds of passage.

Many little birds flock; they tackle the mass of seed that is now ripe and accessible.　Gayest of all are goldfinches on thistle heads.

Hedgehogs begin to hibernate in beds of leaves, but they do not settle down for good, and will come out again on mild evenings.

Several of our mammals scarcely hibernate, but sleep in sheltered places, or their holes during bad weather—badgers (who hibernate fully in the north), squirrels, shrews, and voles are among the animals that behave in this way.

Badger

Moles dig down deeper into the earth. Our Carnivora — stoats, weasels, martens, otters, polecats, and foxes—hunt throughout the winter.

Rabbits, of course, never cease their activities. We are told that they do breed less freely in the late autumn.

On sunny days flies come out again, and gnat-like creatures dance in sunbeams. An occasional butterfly wakes from its hibernation, and one or two moths are about, including the mottled umber. The November moth proper, *Oporinia dilutata*, is a dreary enough creature well suited to the month.

A sunny morning and a thrush singing may delude us for a moment that November is not the cool, still, foggy month that it is reputed to be. But these unseasonable signs are not genuine. All of them will completely disappear for a spell before they reappear at their proper place in the yearly cycle of nature.

ANNIVERSARIES OF EVENTS, EPOCHS, AND RECORDS

5th November 1688. At the beginning of the century Guy Fawkes attempted to blow up the Houses of Parliament and failed; in this year another plot, this time to get rid of the king, came to a head and shortly succeeded. William of Orange arrived from Holland, and landed at Torbay, his army being brought ashore expeditiously and without incident. James II was deserted by most of his followers, and he was tactfully allowed to escape and never returned closer than Ireland. William and Mary—it was Mary who got William the invitation, for prior to the birth of a son to James she was heir to the throne—were crowned, and as not infrequently happens from time to time we acquired a new king from outside our borders. He brought the Dutch fashions of formality with him, which left their mark on the history of our taste.

8th November 1828. Thomas Bewick 'gently sighed away his last breath at half-past one in the morning.' This sturdy, honest Tynesider comes into our almanac—first, as the finest craftsman in wood-engraving that we possess, and then as an artist, who, in his engravings, gave us some of the loveliest (and liveliest) little pictures of the English scene that have ever been made. Sometimes these take the form of daily happenings, at others, that of backgrounds to his famous series of engravings of beasts and birds. He was born in 1753 and spent most of his life around Newcastle.

14th November 1635. Old Parr, who lived most of his long life at Alberbury, near Shrewsbury, died in London aged 152. He attributed his great age, which we claim as our November record, to a liking for green cheese and onions.

14th November 1896. The Locomotives on Highway Act came into force. From this day on self-propelled vehicles had no longer to be accompanied along the road by a pedestrian.

15th November 1837. Isaac Pitman's *Stenographic Sound-Hand* was published by Samuel Bagster of London, price fourpence. Very soon this system and others that followed became widely used, until to-day the stenographer forms a principal part of our younger female population.

21st November 1695. Henry Purcell died, by some held to be the greatest of our English composers. Comparatively rare as are the performances of his works, each one confirms this assessment—which seems to have been accepted quite early on in his short but richly productive life. He was a Londoner, born in 1659. He so often celebrated occasions, from a king's birthday to St. Cecilia's Day, in glorious music, that the almanacker may, perhaps, be allowed a modest wish that his works will before long more frequently be allowed to transfer their fame from the study to the wider spaces of the concert hall.

24th November 1859. Charles Darwin's *Origin of Species* was published. The first edition of 1,250 copies sold out within the day. So few books have so violently revolutionized man's thought that we can be in no doubt in claiming its impact on the world as our November epoch-maker.

29th November 1814. The Times newspaper was first printed on a press driven by a steam-engine. A leader said: 'A system of machinery, almost organic, has been devised and arranged which, while it relieves the human frame of its most laborious efforts in printing, far exceeds all human powers in rapidity and despatch.'

THE POET

If Thomas Hood was an apostle of the school which regards the month as one of unrelieved gloom, his contemporary, the sporting poet R. E. Egerton Warburton, took a violently opposed view:

> Boys, to the hunting-field, though 'tis November,
> The wind's in the south—but a word ere we start,
> Though keenly excited, I bid you remember
> That hunting's a science, and riding an art.

A good many more verses in the same spirit make it quite clear to us that for those who think and feel like Warburton November is the most joyous month of the year.

A compromise is found in John Keble's lines from *The Christian Year*:

> Red o'er the forest peers the setting sun;
>   The line of yellow light dies fast away
> That crown'd the eastern copse; and chill and dun
>   Falls on the moor the brief November day.
>
> Now the tired hunter winds a parting note,
>   And Echo bids good-night from every glade;
> Yet wait awhile and see the calm leaves float
>   Each to his rest beneath their parent shade.

How like decaying life they seem to glide
   And yet no second spring have they in store;
But where they fall, forgotten to abide
   Is all their portion, and they ask no more.

Soon o'er their heads blithe April airs shall sing,
   A thousand wild flowers round them shall unfold,
The green buds glisten in the dews of Spring,
   And all be vernal rapture as of old. . . .

The theme that out of the death of November arises the resurrection of April is developed at length: the leaves, Keble points out, fall and have no further hope (what the 'compost' school of agriculture thinks of this idea I dare not imagine), while the future of man after death is far more full of promise.

There are many pictures of November. Maurice Baring quotes this scene of Crabbe's as an example of the perfect landscape in English poetry—a placid view of calm, resignedly awaiting winter's storms:

There was a day, ere yet the autumn dozed,
When, ere her wintry wars, the earth reposed,
When from the yellow weed the feathery crown,
Light as the curling smoke, fell slowly down;
When the wing'd insect settled in our sight,
And waited wind to recommence her flight;
When the wide river was a silver sheet,
And on the ocean slept th' unanchor'd fleet.

To set against this there is Robert Nichols's picture of the countryside at its gloomiest:

As I walk the misty hill
All is languid, fogged, and still;
Not a note of any bird
Nor any motion's hint is heard,
Save from soaking thickets round
Trickle or water's rushing sound,
And from ghostly trees the drip
Of runnel dews or whispering slip
Of leaves, which in a body launch
Listlessly from the stagnant branch
To strew the marl, already strown,
With litter sodden as its own.

A rheum, like blight, hangs on the briars,
And from the clammy ground suspires
A sweet frail sick autumnal scent
Of stale frost furring weeds long spent;
And wafted on, like one who sleeps,
A feeble vapour hangs or creeps,
Exhaling on the fungus mould
A breath of age, fatigue, and cold.

Oozed from the bracken's desolate track,
By dark rains havocked and drenched black,
A fog about the coppice drifts,
Or slowly thickens up and lifts
Into the moist, despondent air.
Mist, grief, and stillness everywhere. . . .

This in its turn is offset by John Freeman's gentle and happy:

Than these November skies
Is no sky lovelier.   The clouds are deep;
Into their gray the subtle spies
Of colour creep,
Changing that high austerity to delight,
Till even the leaden interfolds are bright.
And, where the cloud breaks, faint far azure peers
Ere a thin flushing cloud again
Shuts up that loveliness, or shares.
The huge great clouds move slowly, gently, as
Reluctant the quick sun should shine in vain,
Holding in bright caprice their rain.
      And when of colours none,
Not rose, nor amber, nor the scarce late green,
Is truly seen—
In all the myriad gray,
In silver height and dusky deep, remain
The loveliest,
Faint purple flushes of the unvanquished sun.

Many poets have sung at some length in honour of St. Cecilia, and it would be invidious to make a choice.   So we will omit them and end with Canon Dixon's *Song*—greatly admired by Robert Bridges—which I think rightly belongs to November.

The feathers of the willow
Are half of them grown yellow
　　Above the swelling stream;
And ragged are the bushes,
And rusty now the rushes,
　　And wild the clouded gleam.

The thistle now is older,
His stalk begins to moulder,
　　His head is white as snow;
The branches all are barer,
The linnet's song is rarer,
　　The robin pipeth now.

DECEMBER  SAGITTARIUS

DECEMBER, the twelfth and last month of our year, has thirty-one days. It was the tenth, hence *decem*, of the ancient Romans.

Anglo-Saxons called it Wintermonath, winter month, or Haligmonath, holy month.

Dark and mysterious, it includes the winter solstice, with its magic calm. On the seven days before and the seven days after the sun moves from Sagittarius to Capricornus, the halcyon birds—which we know as kingfishers—bred on the ocean. During that time no wind blew and the seas were placid.

December, too, miraculously holds both quiet and final death, as well as the first germs of life within its span when

flowers depart,
To see their Mother-root, when they have blown;
Where they together,
All the hard weather,
Dead to the world, keep house unknown.

The spirit of the season has long been celebrated in the northern part of the world. It was wild and exaggerated in Rome's Saturnalia. But the symbolism of giving presents in friendship and making slaves the equal of their masters was there. It developed in a more subtle form in Christmastide, still the greatest of our festivals. The house becomes the centre of the feast.

When that is once over we see for the first time the first, tired face of Janus looking towards us. Then, in a few days, we advance and pass him. The other, a keen young face, is now looking, but in the same direction as our own gaze, with anticipation into a new year, as yet empty.

THE WEATHER

December is usually the dullest and wettest month of the year.   Seldom is it the coldest.   Except in the north and on high ground little snow falls. 'Green' Christmases seem to be much more frequent than 'seasonable' ones.

The normal temperature is between 40° F. and 41° F.

Buchan has his third and final warm spell from the 3rd to the 14th.

There have been a number of exceptionally warm Decembers.   In 1843 the season was so mild that on the 30th apple-trees were reported in bud and even blossom, while polyanthus, wallflowers, daisies, and primroses were in flower.

Most weather sayings are concerned with the ill consequences of a mild or wet Christmastide, both to mankind and the ensuing year.

THE HEAVENS

On about 22nd December the sun passes from Sagittarius into the sign of Capricornus, the Goat.   In so doing it reaches the nadir of its power, giving us the winter solstice and shortest day.   In London this is almost eight and a quarter hours long.   When it is passed the sun begins his ascent to glory, and once more the time of daylight lengthens.

On the 13th or the 14th falls the earliest sunset.   The evenings then begin to draw out.   The sun still rises a little later day by day until the New Year.

FEASTS, FAIRS, AND FESTIVALS

6th December.   St. Nicholas.   Bishop.

Nicholas of Patara was Bishop of Myra in Asia Minor during the fourth century.   He was persecuted and imprisoned for his faith at the time of Diocletian, but not martyred.   He was granted to his parents as a consequence of their earnest prayers; his piety was apparent almost from birth—as an infant he fasted regularly on Wednesdays and Fridays.   When left without parents he dedicated the rest of his life to God.

He miraculously brought together the dismembered parts of the bodies of three schoolboys which had been hidden by their murderer, an innkeeper, in a pickling tub. He also provided bars of gold for three daughters of a man who had lost all his money and, having previously failed to find them husbands, had decided that they should live lives of shame.

These and other stories of his love of children made him very popular, and he was early adopted as the patron of boys and scholars.

In the north his festival coincided with that of the famous old pagan Woden, who rode about the skies and mysteriously distributed gifts. So Nicholas, at the behest of the Church, got himself a team of reindeer and a sledge, moved his home to the clouds and snows of the Arctic, and became Santa Claus.

His emblem is either three purses or balls of gold or sometimes three children. He has no connection with Old Nick.

At one time it was quite usual in cathedrals, some churches and schools to elect a 'boy bishop' on this day. He had his chaplain and other officers, who served until Childermas. Some accounts say that the whole proceeding was nothing more than a burlesque, but in some places at least the children were rigorously controlled, and woe betide them if they got out of hand.

The idea has been successfully revived quite recently.

21st December. St. Thomas. *Apostle and Martyr.*

This apostle symbolizes the affectionate type of man, willing and eager, but slow in apprehending the true significance of things. For this reason he was vouchsafed the most indisputable evidence of the Resurrection—and so (according to tradition) was honoured with an early place in the Church calendar.

Legend says that he went on a mission to India, where he met King Gundaphorus. Thomas had been an architect, so this king of the Indies gave him a vast sum of money to build a palace. Thomas spent it on the poor, and said that he had erected a superb palace in heaven.

His emblem is a square; he is patron of masons and architects.

His day is 'gooding' day. In Herefordshire gleaners could ask for a quartern of corn from the farmer. In other counties, women went 'a-gooding,' 'a-Thomasing,' or 'curning' from house to house to collect doles of wheat which was ground free by the millers so that they could make cakes for Christmas. Sometimes the donor received a sprig of holly or mistletoe in reward.

In some churches it was long customary to take a collection for the poor on the Sunday nearest to St. Thomas's Day.

24th December. Christmas Eve.

The festival of Christmas comes at the end of Advent, days of awaiting the most joyful feast of the Christian year. At last, on Christmas Eve, all final preparations are made for the great day. Churches and homes are decorated. Once evergreens were hung outside houses, but this practice died out, to be revived in a rather different manner by the big stores, who bedeck their façades and hang thousands of little coloured lights, and so add a sparkle to our dull cities.

Holly and ivy are the traditional evergreens, though ivy has now dropped right out of fashion. Holly is symbolic of the crown of thorns splashed with the blood-red of its berries. These traditional plants have long been approved by the Church, but mistletoe, our other Christmas decoration, the golden bough of the ancients, remains an unblessed pagan.

Formerly the centre of the decorations in the home was a kissing bough. Skill and tradition played their part in its construction. Evergreens were twined around a frame and a large bunch of mistletoe usually formed the lower part. This work of art was treated with the respect that it deserved, but has now been replaced by a ragged bunch of mistletoe casually hung on the end of a string.

To-day the Christmas tree is given pride of place. It is quite a newcomer in our long Christmas history, coming from the lands of the north, where fir and spruce—indeed, Christmas trees—grow naturally. Queen Victoria and Prince Albert started its popular career, though it had been seen here before the German prince displayed one to his children. Now it provides a good market for the thinnings of our own conifer forests—which, of course, did not exist in the good old days. Covered with coloured lights (the amateur electrician comes into his own), strings of tinsel, and glittering stars (the largest represents the Star of Bethlehem), it is, indeed, a most lovely sight.

In olden days a Lord of Misrule was appointed to take charge of the ceremonies. In the universities, the Inns of Court, and the City of London he was a person of some consequence. He had special charge of the mummers who went round acting their antique plays with their crowd of stock characters —St. Georges, dragons, Turkish knights, doctors with large boxes of pills, and hobby horses, with musicians to accompany them.

The waits (then instrumentalists) and carol singers started their tours.

So the scene was, and in a different way still is, set for Christmas, a most ancient festival in the lands of the long, dark winters of the north. Long before the coming of Christ evergreens reassured man that the green of life, and bonfires that the warmth of the sun's light, had not gone for ever. It has for that reason always been a festival of joy, though the eternal followers of gloom, especially our own puritans, have had many a try to damp its joyousness. But they have failed, and to-day, aided by the ingenuities of modern commerce though it is, Christmas remains our most joyful feast and holiday.

25th December.   Christmas Day.

This now begins with opening stockings mysteriously filled overnight by Santa Claus (or old St. Nicholas), who drives over the snow-clouds in his sleigh drawn by reindeer and enters houses by the chimney. Though long known on the continent of Europe he has only taken to visiting us quite recently. Our own Father Christmas with his bag of presents has, however, been with us for hundreds of years, and took part in the old mummer's plays.

Next comes the opening of envelopes with their Christmas cards (if this has not been done already). They are very new arrivals, first appearing sometime in the eighteen-sixties. Even so they soon made their own tradition —bright-breasted robins in the snow, and scenes taking us back to the good old days, are their subjects. Even later is the joyful practice of our post office, which uses a postmark of holly leaves—though this does sometimes decorate the envelope bearing our income-tax demands.

Then follows the giving of Christmas presents. Though cards may be opened and proudly arranged around the room before this day, present-parcels must not be touched until it arrives. This custom of present-giving is one of the oldest in Christmas history.

At church, and indeed around the houses, carols are sung. In Georgian times this practice was falling into disuse. The words and tunes were fast disappearing when fortunately the Victorians became interested in them. Like so much else the tunes and words of the oldest were originally of popular secular origin, which the wise old Roman Church adapted for Christian use.

In olden days there was the custom of bringing in, and on Christmas Day, burning the Yule log or faggot. (Yule, of course, is another pagan relic—the name of the festival of the winter solstice.) As it burned, master, family, and servants all sat down together to feast at the Christmas board.

Boar's head was the traditional dish. The turkey, brought into this country in the sixteenth century, has now quite replaced it. Plum-puddings, mince-pies, and all manner of spices, sweets, and fruit were, as now, eaten.

In the evening games were played. Snapdragon was brought in—a dish of raisins to be snatched from the quiet, blue, flickering flames of the burning brandy in which they stood.

So Christmas Day passed—a symbol to all of joyous birth.

26th December.   St. Stephen.   Martyr.   Boxing Day.

Stephen was a great preacher soon after the death of Christ; his insistence on the gulf between Christianity and the old Mosaic institutions aroused the opposition of the sanhedrim. He was stoned to death, and became the first man to suffer martyrdom for his faith in Christ.

The origin of the name Boxing Day is obscure; it has been said that while Christmas Day was an occasion for present-giving between members of the family and friends, on St. Stephen's feast they were given to a wider circle. A century ago there was a move to abolish the gift of Christmas boxes to tradesmen, officials, and so on. It has progressed but little during the intervening years.

In towns a great occasion is the first night of the pantomime—perhaps the survival of the spirit of the mummers' play. This is the first of the post-Christmas entertainments to get off the mark: circuses, parties, and lectures for children and young people fill the next week or two.

27th December.   St. John.   Apostle and Evangelist.

This picturesque and legendary character has already had one miraculous event in his life—survival after being immersed in boiling oil—celebrated on 6th May. After that, at least according to several famous painters, he retired to the island of Patmos, where he kept a tame eagle and wrote the Book of Revelations.

His emblem is a chalice from which emerges a serpent. This symbolizes his power to drive poisons from the cups offered to him by his enemies.

Once he miraculously appeared to two English pilgrims during a crusade and speedily wafted them back to Barham Down in Kent.

28th December. Innocents' Day or Childermas.

This commemorates Herod's butchery of children over two years old dwelling in Bethlehem, in the hope that he would destroy the infant Jesus. This dreadful happening does not seem to have attracted folklore or legend.

31st December. New Year's Eve.

Except in the north, where it is called Hogmanay, this occasion has lost most of its former glory.

It was once the great occasion for wassailing or health-drinking, though this was also a Twelfth Night festivity.

Wassailing of apple-trees was carried on in the cider counties and the south until the last century. For instance, at Haslemere the wassailers met round an old apple-tree, rapped it with sticks, and shouted:

> Here stands a good old apple-tree; stand fast root;
> Every little twig bear an apple big,
> Hats full, caps full, and three-score sacks full,
> Hip! hip! hurrah!

Then followed three loud blasts on a horn.

Perhaps the only relic of this ceremonial drinking lingers on in those households which brew usually noxious punch for the occasion.

The pagan rites of this season were long frowned on by the Church, but being cheerful in nature they persisted. So in the eighth century the Church made the best of a bad job and turned the first day of the new year—the new year of the people, not of lawyers—into a festival in honour of the Circumcision. So a respectable look was given to the calendar of January, and people could celebrate the arrival of the two-faced god in a new way by going to church on the vigil of Circumcision. In some churches a watch-night service is still held, and the bells pealed immediately after midnight.

Most people still have a feeling of awe and wonder as the approach of another year draws near, in spite of our vaunted assumption of a rational and scientific outlook. Even at this day, it is placated, perhaps jokingly, by lingering superstition. A dark man (preferably a stranger, or if not he should be masked) must be the first to cross the threshold after the last stroke of twelve has struck. He knocks at the door; right of entry is his and cannot be delayed. He bears propitiatory gifts which he carries through the house —coal, bread, or money are brought according to the custom in the locality. If no fair man precedes him, and all goes well as he makes his round, then good luck will stay in the house throughout the year just begun.

And so we turn back to January and start all over again.

THE SPORTSMAN

The only date in the sporting calendar is the tenth, when the shooting of grouse, ptarmigan, and black grouse ends.

At Christmas time there are usually some good football matches, and throughout the month fox hunting is in full swing; children's meets are held during the holidays.

Otherwise there are few events, and we should, perhaps, refer to some more of our omissions throughout the year. These consist mostly of the newer, mechanically contrived sports. Their seasons, if they have any, depend on the weather of the country in which they are held, for they are international and by no means British, though our people are passable performers at some of them. Such are motor racing—rather spasmodic and commercialized; cycle and motor-cycle racing, both on road circuits and on dirt-tracks— made possible by the invention and development of the pneumatic tyre in the eighteen-nineties, or aeroplane racing—again largely a matter of commercial and even international prestige.

Then there is greyhound racing, a form of gambling on the pursuit of a mechanical hare by highly trained dogs.

Or athletics—whose important events are prone to occur at what appear to be most unpropitious seasons. And there are subtle games like tennis and fives, or the more popular squash rackets, whose seasons are rather vaguely defined.

And indeed many other sports—for who shall deny that marbles is a sport, or top-spinning as skilled as many a game? All have their seasons. But I cannot find them in any official calendar so they must be left out.

Then there is mountaineering, or, in a more modest form, rock and fell climbing. Is that a sport or only an arduous pursuit? We are told that the conquest of the Matterhorn by Sir Arthur Wills in 1854 gave it prominence and started its popularity, which has grown enormously since the formation of the Alpine Club in 1858. We might guess that Easter is about the opening of the season because that is about the time of year when men of all ages and young women, oddly attired and bearing large quantities of rope, are first noticed in the hotels of our more mountainous districts.

But it is not for the almanacker to define sport; he, therefore, ends the year with an apology to those enthusiasts whose particular pet date in the calendar remains unrecorded.

THE NATURALIST

An apparently lifeless month, when there is little to see or do out of doors.

I suppose that in olden times the naturalists spent their evenings, lit by oil or even gas lamps, arranging their vast collections of camphor-scented butter-flies and moths, or classifying drawers full of musty-smelling birds' eggs. To-day, I presume, they sit, their eyes shaded by green bands from powerful electric lights, voluminous notes on one side, and Professor Fisher's book about statistical systems for research workers on the other, and settle them-selves down to a nice evening sorting out the problems of nature (of course, they don't call it that) by arithmetic.

Perhaps this is better than exterminating wild life to provide specimens. Fortunately the old type of naturalist, a man of wide interests, is still allowed to exist. It is true that he may have to do quite a bit of measuring and counting, as well as some mathematics. Above all he must remember to call himself an *ecologist*. But providing he does this he may continue un-harmed and undespised to observe natural life amid its environment. With luck he will avoid achieving that dreadful fate, dying an acknowledged expert on—well, anything you, reader, dislike.

In December there is an absence of distracting detail which makes both easier and interesting an attempt to observe things as a whole. One may realize some of the foolish ideas that are often held. Such, for example, is the attempt to separate 'wild' or 'native' nature (whatever that may be, for definition, other than as a generalization, is not easy) from what is, I suppose, 'tame' or 'exotic' nature. In a small place like the British Isles the impact of man on 'nature' is almost as widespread as that of 'nature' on man. The border-land where these two meet— farms, gardens, suburbia, parks, forests (which are largely man-made)—covers a great part of our islands, and forms possibly the most interesting ground for study.

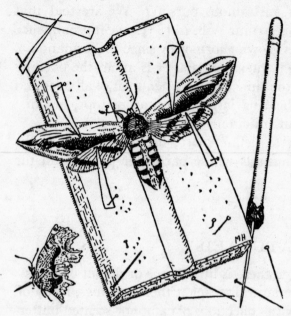

The Lepidopterist's Table

It is in woodlands, forests, and among trees—usually considered lovely wild places—that the influence of man is paramount. Of those big evergreens which now warm and solidify the winter landscape, and which (except for coniferous plantations) are accepted as an integral part of the English scene, few, except yew, holly, and to a very small extent Scots pine, were here a century or two ago.

A few maintain themselves and increase without assistance. But most do not. Few trees are more typical of English parkland than the Wellingtonia. Yet it was not even discovered by scientists until 1841, and first raised in England in 1853. The vogue for planting this majestic green spire has died out; it does not reproduce itself in this country, and will, therefore, gradually disappear.

There is, too, much ill-informed criticism of the way poor, thin-soiled hill-sides are afforested with conifers. Much of the opposition is because they are 'foreign' species. Such critics are prone to talk lovingly, even to write poems, about the Balkan horse-chestnuts, and regard with pleasure and indeed make tasteful pencil sketches of the dear old London planes, of sycamores, sweet chestnuts, and walnuts, which are but a few of the trees introduced from abroad. Many conifers grew here in prehistoric times—including a relative of the Wellingtonia—and their disappearance is largely an accident of geography.

The natural history of weeds and insects introduced in the process of cultivation, the intimate botanical connection between garden and wild plants, and the reckless disregard shown by many birds and most insects for the walls and fences put up by man, all demonstrate forcibly that there is as much natural history in a suburban plot as there is in some remote Hebridean isle.

But what are the features of December itself? Many mosses, lichens, liverworts, and fungi are

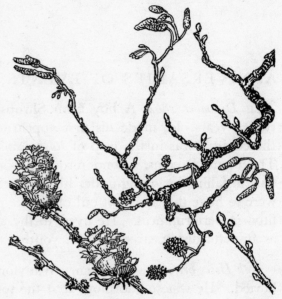

Larch and Alder

in their prime and awaiting study—thriving as all else disappears. Mixed flocks of birds move gregariously around the country now, quite unhidden by foliage. Cones are ripening—some crack open and others disintegrate leaving only their central spike. Catkins of birch will be scattering their seed by disintegration; alders, by opening their valves.

The romantic-sounding Glastonbury thorn, to the botanist merely *Crataegus monogyna biflora*, will be giving its first winter round of bloom wherever it has been planted, providing the weather is suitable. It flowers again in summer.

Several winter moths, drab-winged males and crawling females, best seen when trapped on the gummy bands tied round the trunks of fruit trees, will be abroad in the evenings—so ingeniously escaping many foes.

As the winter solstice arrives it is in the woods that there is confirmation that spring will come and life revive once again. Sticky horse-chestnut buds can be cut through to display the embryo flower. Birches and alders are covered with small, tight-rolled catkins; on pines young green cones will be developing. On the hazels the catkins will be even larger. And they will open in January. And January is . . . only next month!

ANNIVERSARIES OF EVENTS, EPOCHS, AND RECORDS

1st December 1804. A boy from Shropshire, William West Betty, scarcely twelve years old, made his first appearance on the London stage. Shortly the country was in the grip of *Rosciomania*, and Betty had achieved fame as The Young Roscius. London society followed the ironworkers of Coalbrookdale in falling headlong under his spell; crowds attending to see him perform were so huge that they got out of hand. At one time he made £34,000 from fifty-six performances. He lived to the age of eighty-four but his reputation as an actor disappeared with his youth.

10th December 1741. Mr. Henry Wanyford, steward to the Earl of Essex, was buried. He was so enormous that the top had to be taken off the hearse to get his body into it, while his coffin was so heavy that rollers were needed to move it. He vies with a wasp in creating our December record.

13th December 1577. The *Golden Hind*, at the head of her little fleet, commanded by Francis Drake, sailed from Plymouth on a voyage which was to become famous as the first circumnavigation of the globe by Englishmen. She returned on 26th September 1580 laden with gold, spices, pearls, amber, and silks. The politicians, no doubt under the advice of the officials of the day, hesitated to recognize this event (which we celebrate as our December epoch-maker) for fear that the King of Spain might be peeved; no doubt 'after the most careful consideration of all the circumstances they were of the opinion that notwithstanding . . .' until Elizabeth went down to Deptford, had a banquet on board the *Golden Hind*, and afterwards knighted Drake.

19th December 1848. A number of eminent persons inspected the new gas-meter for the Houses of Parliament. Far exceeding in dimensions and artistry anything before attempted, this 'almost stupendous piece of mechanism' was in the form of a hexagon, ten feet high, and designed in the Gothic manner. It was, therefore, an ornamental as well as a useful addition to the Houses. The castings of the ornamentation were remarkably sharp and included the name of the patentee, the title of the Chartered Gas Company, and the royal arms.

19th December 1851. J. M. W. Turner died in Chelsea. Son of a barber, he was born in London on St. George's Day 1775. Perhaps the greatest painter of land, sky, and sea that has ever lived, he was a bit of a tough at heart, and no doubt to escape from being swamped by the cult of the genteel he lived double lives. The best known of these was as Mr. Booth the husband of his Margate landlady.

Continuously successful from his early days he died worth about £140,000.

20th December 1947. Mr. L. G. Carter was playing golf on the Henbury course at Bristol when he was stung under the chin by a wasp. This competes with the enormous Mr. Wanyford as our December record.

24th December. No English almanac would be complete without some reference to Robin Hood. He was, it seems, several people, but we will choose one who died on this day to commemorate them all.

Robin Hood, therefore, died in 1247, after a minor operation which went wrong. It was at Kirklee Priory Farm, Yorkshire, that he bled to death at the age of eighty-seven.

29th December 1197. Thomas à Becket, archbishop, was murdered in his own cathedral at Canterbury. It is related that he had previously dined on pheasant, 'more heartily and cheerfully on that day than usual.' The tale is well known—how a party of knights, anxious to curry favour with Henry II, slew the archbishop, largely through a misunderstanding. The murder made Thomas a European hero, and many miraculous legends sprung up around his name; Canterbury, too, became famous as the centre of what the experts now call 'a saint-hero cult.'

THE POET

Without doubt Keats must come first:

> In a drear-nighted December,
>   Too happy, happy tree,
> Thy branches ne'er remember
>   Their green felicity:
> The north cannot undo them;
> With a sleety whistle through them;
> Nor frozen thawings glue them
>   From budding at the prime.
>
> In a drear-nighted December,
>   Too happy, happy brook,
> Thy bubblings ne'er remember
>   Apollo's summer look;
> But with a sweet forgetting,
> They stay their crystal fretting,
> Never, never petting
>   About the frozen time.
>
> Ah! would 'twere so with many
>   A gentle girl and boy!
> But were there ever any
>   Writhed not at passèd joy?
> To know the change and feel it,
> When there is none to heal it,
> Nor numbèd sense to steal it,
>   Was never said in rhyme.

Next we can place Samuel Johnson's unhappy winter confession:

> Behold, my fair, where'er we rove,
>   What dreary prospects round us rise;
> The naked hill, the leafless grove,
>   The hoary ground, the frowning skies!
> Nor only through the wasted plain,
>   Stern Winter! is thy force confess'd;
> Still wider spreads thy horrid reign,
>   I feel thy power usurp my breast.

Enlivening hope, and fond desire,
   Resign the heart to spleen and care;
Scarce frighted Love maintains her fire,
   And rapture saddens to despair.
In groundless hope, and causeless fear,
   Unhappy man! behold thy doom;
Still changing with the changeful year,
   The slave of sunshine and of gloom.
Tir'd with vain joys, and false alarms,
   With mental and corporeal strife,
Snatch me, my Stella, to thy arms,
   And hide me from the sight of life.

For a December landscape there are the lines from Scott's *Marmion*:

When dark December glooms the day,
And takes our autumn joys away;
When short and scant the sunbeam throws,
Upon the weary waste of snows,
A cold and profitless regard,
Like patron on a needy bard;
When silvan occupation 's done,
And o'er the chimney rests the gun,
And hang, in idle trophy, near,
The game-pouch, fishing-rod, and spear;
When wiry terrier, rough and grim,
And greyhound, with his length of limb,
And pointer, now employ'd no more,
Cumber our parlour's narrow floor;
When in his stall the impatient steed
Is long condemn'd to rest and feed;
When from our snow-encircled home
Scarce cares the hardiest step to roam,
Since path is none, save that to bring
The needful water from the spring;
When wrinkled news-page, thrice conn'd o'er,
Beguiles the dreary hour no more ...

Which with Scott-like lack of haste leads up to the conclusion that in December the city is preferable to the country.

There is no space to quote from the extensive poetry of Christmas, but so that it is not entirely neglected a verse from Frederick Tennyson's *The Holy Tide* may be quoted:

> The days are sad, it is the Holy tide:
>   Be dusky mistletoes and hollies strown,
> Sharp as the spear that pierced His sacred side,
>   Red as the drops upon His thorny crown;
> No haggard Passion and no lawless Mirth
>   Fright off the solemn Muse—tell old sweet tales,
> Sing songs as we sit brooding o'er the hearth,
>   Till the lamp flickers, and the memory fails.

Some of the feelings and traditions connected with awaiting the coming year are also appropriate to December, and may be represented by Sir Arthur Quiller-Couch's *Upon New Year's Eve*:

> Now winds of winter glue
>   Their tears upon the thorn,
> And earth has voices few,
>   And those forlorn.
>
> And 'tis our solemn night
>   When maidens sand the porch
> And play at *Jack's Alight*
>   With burning torch,
>
> Or cards, or *Kiss i' the Ring*—
>   While ashen faggots blaze,
> And late wassailers sing
>   In miry ways.
>
> Then, dear my wife, be blithe
>   To bid the New Year hail
> And welcome—plough, drill, scythe,
>   And jolly flail.
>
> For though the snows he'll shake
>   Of winter from his head,
> To settle, flake by flake,
>   On ours instead;

Yet we be wreathed green
  Beyond his blight or chill,
Who kiss'd at seventeen,
  And worship still.

We know not what he 'll bring;
  But this we know to-night—
He doth prepare the Spring
  For our delight.

With birds he 'll comfort us,
  With blossoms, balms, and bees,
With brooks, and odorous
  Wild breath o' the breeze.

Come then, O festal prime!
  With sweets thy bosom fill
And dance, dripping thyme,
  On Lantick hill.

West wind awake! and comb
  Our garden blade from blade—
We, in our little home,
  Sit unafraid.

So far we have been solemn; let us, therefore, turn to the eighteenth century and Christopher Smart's *Ode on the Fifth of December, being the Birthday of a beautiful young Lady*:

Hail, eldest of the monthly train,
  Sire of the winter drear,
December, in whose iron reign
  Expires the checker'd year,
Hush all the blustering blasts that blow,
And proudly plum'd in silver snow,
  Smile gladly on this blest of days.
The liveried clouds shall on thee wait,
And Phoebus shine in all his state
  With more than summer rays.

Though jocund June may justly boast
  Long days and happy hours,
Though August be Pomona's host.
  And May be crown'd with flowers;
Tell June, his fire and crimson dyes,
By Harriot's blush and Harriot's eyes
  Eclips'd and vanquish'd, fade away;
Tell August, thou canst let him see
A richer, riper, fruit than he,
  A sweeter flower than May.

And then to end with a sparkling, frosty, white scene by Walter de la Mare:

Green Mistletoe!
Oh, I remember now
A dell of snow,
Frost on the bough;
None there but I:
Snow, snow, and a wintry sky.

None there but I,
And footprints one by one,
Zigzaggedly,
Where I had run;
Where shrill and powdery
A robin sat in the tree.

And he whistled sweet;
And I in the crusted snow
With snow-clubbed feet
Jigged to and fro,
Till, from the day,
The rose-light ebbed away.

And the robin flew
Into the air, the air,
The white mist through;
And small and rare
The night-frost fell
Into the calm and misty dell.

And the dusk gathered low,
And the silver moon and stars
On the frozen snow
Drew taper bars,
Kindled winking fires
In the hooded briers.

And the sprawling Bear
Growled deep in the sky;
And Orion's hair
Streamed sparkling by:
But the North sighed low,
'Snow, snow, more snow!'

MOVABLE  FEASTS

Plough Sunday.   The First Sunday after Twelfth Day (6th January).

THIS day is symbolical of the return to work after the Christmas holiday (the twelve days of Christmas) and of the start of ploughing as the first step towards the new harvest.   It must nearly always have been symbolical only, as there is very early evidence to show that ploughing was done in autumn.

Of recent years the occasion has been successfully revived in many country churches.   The services, for which a plough is usually brought into the church, have been well supported by young people.

Plough Monday.

This very ancient festival, held on the day after Plough Sunday, once celebrated in a worldly way the return to the plough after Christmas.   The youths of the villages, dressed in white shirts and wearing gay ribbons at their shoulders, dragged a plough to the village green.   Then followed a ritual sword dance, which ended with the 'killing' of a fool or jester.   This is said to be a relic of an even earlier celebration which concluded with a ritual murder.

The custom has almost entirely died out; at times the sword dance has rather self-consciously been revived.

Septuagesima.   The third Sunday before Lent.

So called because in round numbers it is some seventy days (actually nine weeks) before Easter Sunday.

Sexagesima.   The second Sunday before Lent.

In round numbers sixty days (actually eight weeks) before Easter Sunday.

Little tradition seems to be attached either to this or to the preceding festival.

Quinquagesima or Shrove Sunday. The Sunday next before Lent.

Called Quinquagesima because it falls roughly fifty days before Easter. It is the last Sunday before Lent, a period of fasting once rigorously maintained. No meat, eggs, or even butter could be eaten. Under the simple economy of our forefathers this made the fast a real hardship.

Shrovetide was, therefore, the occasion when the people went to confession, and were shriven prior to a long period of abstemiousness.

Collop Monday. The day after Shrove Sunday.

In olden times this was the day when all the remaining meat in the house was cut into collops or steaks, so that it could be preserved by drying or salting until the end of Lent. It became traditional to eat eggs and collops or eggs and bacon for dinner on this day. The custom may still linger on in some country places.

Shrove Tuesday. The seventh Tuesday before Easter Day.

We now come to one of those occasions on which pagan rites and Christian festival became merged—or nearly so—and have left us with a complex mass of tradition.

The pagan element was the traditional and often licentious heathen *Fornacalia* of Rome, which took place in February. This was later opposed by the long Christian fast of Lent, which began at about the same time of the year. In the end, of course, the Church adapted and modified most of the pagan customs to suit its own ways.

Shrove Tuesday was the eve of Lent. In the days when our Church was but one and Roman, the people went to confess and be shriven. At the same time it was the last day for eating butter and fat, and so pancakes were made to mark the occasion. As it was immediately prior to Ash Wednesday and not a holy day or fast, odd relics of the *Fornacalia* such as games of football became attached to it.

The spirit of the Roman feast was licence and riotousness. To some extent this maintained in English Shrovetide customs for many centuries. It was the practice for schoolboys to bar the schoolroom against the master; if he failed to get in the day was a holiday. It was, too, often a holiday for that other class of riotous youth, the apprentices.

P

The day began with the ringing of a bell, and ended similarly. Between the bells games and riotous joking could go on unhindered. Women rubbed sooty hands on the faces of those they met, boys banged on doors and removed knockers. Cock-fighting was a general sport.

Most interesting are the survivals of football, with their local and peculiar rules. Shrovetide ball games are still played in the main street of Atherstone, at Ashbourne (where streams have to be crossed, and the goals are three miles apart), at Chester-le-Street, and at Sedgefield. At Alnwick the game caused so much damage that it was moved from the streets to a field. At Corfe Castle the game is associated with the court of the Ancient Company of Marblers, and certain rights of way for the carriage of Purbeck marble to the sea. In some places football is replaced by hurling, or hockey-like games.

A little of this sporting element still clings to the pancake. It may be seen in the scramble for a pancake tossed over an iron bar which divides the Lower from the Upper School at Westminster. The boy who gets it, or the greater part of it, is given a guinea. Or in another form it is found in the Olney Pancake Race, which has been run most years since 1445. The competitors are housewives. The church bells first warn them of the time to fry their pancakes, and then, when to go to the starting point, which is the church door. The race is over a quarter-mile course. As they run the competitors must toss their pancakes three times. The winning-post is the village pump, where the runners are awaited by the vicar and the bell-ringer. The first housewife in, who must, of course, have followed the rules, receives her prize —a kiss from the bell-ringer.

Ash Wednesday. The day after Shrove Tuesday, and the first in Lent.

The name comes from the custom of burning last year's consecrated 'palm'—an allegory of the return to dust and ashes of all life.

Lent comes from the Old English and heathen name for spring, but has long been attached to the fast by which the Church commemorates the forty days that Christ spent in the wilderness, and was tempted of the devil.

Mothering Sunday. The fourth or middle Sunday in Lent, and third before Easter Day.

We are told that in the pagan north the Mother of the Gods was honoured at this season. The early Christians diverted the celebrations towards bringing gifts to the Mother Church. Later, under the Protestants, the mother in the home became the object of attention, specially from those children living far away, who bring or send gifts of trinkets or posies of spring flowers.

Simnel cakes are now also associated with Mothering Sunday, but they really recall the first Church lesson of the day, the banquet given by Joseph to his brethren, and the gospel, which tells of the feeding of the five thousand. Perhaps, however, their origin is even earlier and rather more pagan. There are one or two different kinds, the recipes varying from place to place. Those of Lancashire, Devizes, and Bury are particularly famous. At Chilbolton in Hampshire a special wafer, whose secret formula belongs to the Baverstock family, replaces simnel cake.

Passion Sunday. Carle Sunday. The fifth in Lent and second before Easter.

The Church celebrates the Passion of our Lord. The old name of Care, Carle, or Carling Sunday is variously explained. Some say that it refers to the 'care' or sorrow of the Passion, others to the practice of eating peas fried in butter, or 'carle,' supposedly a relic of the pagan bean-feast.

Palm Sunday. The Sunday before Easter.

It is so called as a memorial to Christ's triumphal entry into Jerusalem riding on the back of an ass. The crowds laid palm leaves before him. This was a Roman custom. In northern lands palm has been replaced by sprays of sallow, which open their golden catkins on bare twigs at this season of the year. The name palm has become attached to the shrub.

In the early Church a procession was held symbolizing the entry into Jerusalem. This developed into a pageant, to which the puritan spirit objected, and it was stopped.

Monday, Tuesday, and Wednesday before Easter.

The Church keeps all these days as Holy Days.

Thursday before Easter. Maundy, Chere, or Shere Thursday.

Royal Maundy purses of money are given to as many poor men and poor women as there are years in the king's age. It is a relic of a ceremony celebrating the washing of the feet of the Apostles by Christ. Up to the days of James II the king himself came to Westminster Abbey and washed the feet of the recipients of the gift, but he was the last monarch to do so.

217

Usually the Archbishop of Canterbury distributes the purses after a special service and ceremony which includes symbols of the origin of the gifts. Occasionally the king does it himself.

The word maundy comes from the same root as the word mandate, a command—'A new commandment I give unto you. That ye love one another . . .,' which was spoken after the washing of the disciples' feet.

Good Friday. The Friday before Easter.

On this day the anniversary of Christ's crucifixion is commemorated.

Hot cross buns, spiced buns marked with a cross, were probably eaten at this season of the year long before the coming of Christianity—it seems certain that the Romans had them. They must, of course, be eaten hot from the oven.

A legend still lingers on that bread baked on Good Friday will last throughout the year. Crumbs of it placed in water have remarkable curative properties.

Those born on Good Friday were once reputed to have the power of seeing and commanding spirits.

Marbles is a children's game traditionally associated with Eastertide.

Easter Day.

Since Christ was crucified at full moon during the festival of the Passover this day, on which the movable feasts of the Church depend, is fixed as the first Sunday after the first full moon after the vernal equinox on 21st March. Therefore it can fall on any date as early as 22nd March and not later than 25th April.

Celebrating the Resurrection of Christ it is probably the earliest of Christian festivals. The Church has always celebrated it with great ceremony since its day was finally fixed in 525. Processions, illuminations, and religious plays have been important features of the feast.

But as with most of our great days it has a pagan origin and is, in fact, an adaptation of the rites honouring Eastre, the Saxon goddess of spring and dawn.

Mixture of paganism and Christianity that it may be, it is difficult not to feel keenly the symbolism of Easter. Pitched in the uncertain but lovely spring, it is a festival of the dawn of summer, the rapid revival of life and spirit after the apparent death of winter. It is, indeed, a festival of the rising sun—did not Sir Thomas Browne combat the vulgar error that the sun itself danced as it rose on Easter Day?

Is it not symbolized, too, by that great miracle of birth, the egg? From the earliest times the paschal egg has played its part in the ceremony. (Paschal, the dictionary tells us, is pertaining to the Passover or Easter, coming from the Hebrew *pasakh*, to pass over; our own Easter is a local Saxon name.) These eggs were hen eggs dyed in bright colours, red, green, or yellow, after hard-boiling. The name was generally corrupted to 'pace egg.' Children used to go 'pace-egging' or begging eggs. Egg-rolling games were played.

Our modern Easter eggs, of cardboard or confectionery, are, like Christmas cards, a Victorian invention.

The hare is also connected with Easter celebrations.

In the Roman Church flint and steel are used to strike a 'new fire' with which to light the paschal candle.

On Easter Day everything must be bright and new; spring flowers must decorate church and house (though this is not always so easy as in the days when Easter was nearly a fortnight later). Women must wear new clothes for the morning church service, for if they do not 'crows' will soil the old ones.

Monday and Tuesday in Easter Week.

The Church keeps both of these as holy days, and the State the first as a bank holiday.

There have been a number of odd customs on Easter Monday. In Leicester the mayor and corporation sallied out to 'hunt the hare.' At Thaxted in Essex there is morris dancing. In Kent the Biddenden Dole is given. The income from twenty acres of ground, known as the Bread and Cheese Lands, is used to purchase bread and cheese for the poor. At the same time a thousand more or less inedible Biddenden cakes are given away. The origin of this custom is doubtful. At Haslemere it was the occasion for making a Jack-o'-Lent—an effigy of some person who was generally disliked for a particular characteristic or act was mounted on a donkey. Round its neck was hung a placard announcing the objectionable feature. A procession formed and paraded round until it drew up outside the house of the miserable (or perhaps deserved) victim.

In the south tansy cakes and puddings were eaten until well on in last century. They must have been displeasing, as tansy, although tonic, has a very bitter taste; indeed, it is said that it was used in remembrance of the bitter herbs eaten by the Jews at the Passover.

Hock or Hoke Tide. The Monday and Tuesday following the Sunday after Easter.

Old books say that Hock-day fell on the Tuesday and commemorated the occasion when the English surprised and finally defeated the Danes, and so ended an annoyance that had lasted 255 years. Landlords received an annual tribute from their tenants and serfs for allowing them to celebrate the occasion. Modern authors merely state that the origin of Hocktide is obscure.

The custom seems to have been that on Monday young men carried round a chair and 'lifted' young women, who gave them a kiss in return. The women then did the same for the men on Tuesday. A number of local variations are recorded, and a crude and more boisterous form of the same custom lasted in the north and industrial midlands until well on in the nineteenth century, with the difference that it had been moved to Easter Monday and Tuesday.

A most complex ceremony is performed at Hungerford on Hock Tuesday. It opens with the blowing of a horn made in 1634. Then follows a proclamation calling on the people to attend at the court house. A court of feoffment meets and conducts strange and original business, and finally there is a parade of the Tutti-men, accompanied by the Orange Scrambler. The first carry long poles, decorated with a nosegay and bearing an orange. The Tutti-men demand from every man a coin and from every woman a kiss. If the woman refuses she is fined a penny, but when the kiss is given she takes the orange from the pole. It is at once replaced by the Orange Scrambler.

Rogation Sunday. The fifth Sunday after Easter.

The name, from the Latin *rogare*, to ask, refers to the gospel of the day: 'Hitherto have ye asked nothing in my name: ask, and ye shall receive. . . .'

It is now sometimes celebrated as Farm Sunday; a service is held actually on the farm.

Rogation Days. The Monday, Tuesday, and Wednesday after Rogation Sunday, or before Ascension Day.

Rogationtide, or the Gang-days, were the days for 'ganging' round the parish. There seem to have been two objects underlying the procedure. First, supplication that there may be good crops, and secondly, marking the parish boundaries; in some cases the second is linked with Ascensiontide.

Once again we must look to the Romans for origins. These were the festivals of *Ambarvalia* and *Terminalia*. The *Ambarvalia* took place on the Ides of May in honour of Ceres. Processions went around the ploughed fields and sacrifices were made to ensure that crops prospered and brought a good harvest. *Terminalia* were celebrations in honour of the god Terminus, deity of bounds and limits, who was represented by a stone head without feet or arms to show that once placed he never moved. The connection of this feast with this season is accidental, as we are told that the *Terminalia* were held in February.

Before the Reformation the parish was perambulated with great ceremony. There was fasting, carrying of banners, and many local superstitious practices. At certain points the procession stopped, and the priest read the 104th Psalm: 'Thou hast set them their bounds which they shall not pass. . . .' Prayers were offered for a good harvest.

With the Reformation this procession was stopped, but 'beating the bounds' remained. Schoolboys usually went around, possibly with the priest or the schoolmaster, and beat certain traditional boundary marks with sticks.

There remained much variety and local superstition. Willow twigs, often peeled, were used in some places; at others poles topped with milkwort (*Polygala vulgaris*)—this plant was still known as Rogation-flower during last century. Sometimes one member of the ganging party was set upon— perhaps thrown into a pond—to celebrate the occasion, and subsequently compensated for the discomfort he had suffered. In many cases the boys themselves were bumped or whipped at the marks so that they never forgot the bounds of the parish.

There are too many relics of this custom to enumerate. Examples are St. Clement Danes (where the procession takes to the river), Oxford (several processions—in some there is a scramble for pennies), Lichfield (where the clergy carry elm boughs), and Twyford (where the fields are still blessed).

Ascension Day or Holy Thursday.   The Thursday following Rogation Sunday, or the second before Whitsunday.

On this day is celebrated the anniversary of our Lord's ascent into heaven.

The beating of bounds and riding of marches—similar boundary-marking occasions—usually happening at Rogationtide are to some extent also connected with Ascensiontide.   But probably the most interesting ceremony on this day is well-dressing, which, however, is not confined to it.

In its most elaborate form the well-head is surmounted by skilfully wrought pictures of biblical subjects, framed with more formal decorations.   These are formed from panels of clay into which are pressed flowers, leaves, twigs, bark, and so on—even rice, grains of corn, and the most delicate petals are used to achieve the necessary effect.   Most famous is the Tissington well-dressing, which has often been illustrated, but the practice is still carried on at a number of other places in Derbyshire, Staffordshire, and Gloucestershire. Usually the decorated wells are visited by the clergy and parishioners, who give thanks for the wonderful gift of water, but at Buxton—very dependent on its special wells—the affair is an elaborate civic occasion.

Whitsunday.   The seventh Sunday after Easter.

On this Sunday Pentecost is commemorated.   Originally a Jewish festival fifty days after the Passover, the occasion now celebrates the spiritual or imaginative side of Christianity; as the collect for the day says, 'the light of the Holy Spirit.'

The dictionaries tell us that the name is due to a tradition that made this a favourite season for baptism of children, who were dressed in white.

Whit Monday and Whit Tuesday.   The next days after Whitsunday.

The Church still distinguishes these as holy days; the people have, from very early times, made the first one of the most cheerful holidays of the year, and an official bank holiday it remains.

Whitsuntide was the occasion for the parish supper.   It originated as a communal meal, to which all who came contributed.   Village enemies sat down together, and for this once behaved as friends; no doubt toasts were drunk in Whitsun ale brewed specially for the event.

During medieval times garlanded bowers were set up, processions made, and miracle plays performed.

But it seems to have been particularly noted as the opening of the season for morris dancing. Rather self-consciously, the dance still survives at a few places. It is now quite a long time since Maurice Hewlett wrote of the performance he had seen at Bampton: 'The morris has become a vestige, like the Fyfield elm, of the rudimentary. But I am glad to have seen it.' The vestige still remains, as it does at Headington and a number of other villages.

At Whitsun 'Mr. Robert Dover's Olympic Games upon Cotswold Hills' took place:

> Early in May up got the jolly rout,
> Called by the lark, and spread the fields about . . .

In the time of James I Captain Dover, a Warwickshire attorney, bought himself a house at Stanway on the Cotswolds. On a hill near Chipping Camden he inaugurated these sports—foot and horse racing, and every kind of athletic encounter. A volume of verse was published in their honour in 1636. With Ben Jonson and Drayton among the contributors it made the games and Captain Dover famous. They were revived intermittently, but never successfully, after his death in 1641.

The Trial for the Dunmow Flitch has been held on several dates. Once it was 7th June, while now it seems to be held late in the summer. But for a long time it was an event for Whit Monday. There are medieval records of 'the bacon of Dunmow' which was awarded to the man who could swear before the prior, convent, and villagers of Little Dunmow that he had lived with his wife in 'quiet, peaceable, tender, loving cohabitation for a period of three years.' In olden times few couples qualified. Chaucer refers to the trial, and with a few breaks it has continued to take place ever since. The wife was first allowed her say in the eighteenth century. It has now become a rather hilarious affair. The verdict is given by a jury of six spinsters and six bachelors. The court moves about Essex from year to year and is not always held at Dunmow. The generosity of New Zealand in providing the bacon made a revival possible after the last war.

Lichfield once had to provide armour for the forces and keep it in proper condition. A Court of Array met annually to ensure that this was done. It still meets at Whitsuntide, youths parading in the now antique suits. The ceremony is called Lichfield Bower, and large numbers of colliers from the neighbouring mines, as well as others from the surrounding districts, visit the old city for the occasion.

Trinity Sunday.   The Sunday after Whitsunday.

In the words of the collect for the day this celebration is 'to acknowledge the glory of the eternal Trinity.' Little or no lore has accumulated around this day.

The second Monday after Trinity Sunday was the occasion of the guild show at Shrewsbury—a town still famous to-day for its shows. The guilds rivalled one another in building magnificent arbours to house their displays on a site at Kingsland. Records in the reign of Henry VI tell of the show having been held time out of mind.

Corpus Christi.   The Thursday after Trinity Sunday.

A feast in honour of the host, or consecrated bread of the Eucharist. It is primarily a Roman Catholic festival.

In medieval times this was one of the days on which it was usual to perform mystery plays, though saints' days and in particular Whitsuntide were also chosen.

The famous Chester Mysteries were for long performed on Corpus Christi. They were probably introduced from France by Sir John Arneway in the second half of the thirteenth century. Some twenty-five different plays were used, each with a standard text which was kept by the corporation. All were religious or moral, with broad, comic characters interspersed in knock-about interludes.

Each play was allotted to a different guild, which was responsible for the performance. A gaily decorated wheeled stage was used. This was in two tiers, the lower forming the dressing- and property-room, the upper being the platform on which the action took place.

The whole cycle of plays took three days to perform. It was divided into three series. When at a given spot at the end of the first day the first series had been performed, that guild with its stage moved on elsewhere and another stage was wheeled into position. The same happened at the end of the second day, so that the audience at any one spot could see the whole cycle.

Attendances from the surrounding districts were enormous. The Chester Mysteries were performed for three centuries; for the last hundred years or so the occasion was moved to Whitsun. Eventually Puritan opposition and the cost of production ended their run.

August Bank Holiday.   The first Monday in August.

Here at last is a holiday which did not originate in the times of pagan Rome or even in the early days of the Church. Sir John Lubbock, later Lord

Avebury, introduced his Bank Holidays Bill soon after he entered Parliament in 1870, and the first August 'Banker' was in 1873.

The secretary of the Cutlers' Company of Sheffield is, however, by law compelled to work on this day. Under an Act of Parliament of 1790 he must attend his office on the first Monday of August to select 'twelve assistants' to the company. No member of the company ever attends, there is no quorum, and assistants are selected and elected at the next meeting. But the secretary has to go to his office, just in case.

The First Sunday in Advent. The Sunday nearest to St. Andrew (30th November), either before or after.

The period of Advent really begins the Church year. On its four Sundays are commemorated the coming of Christ to earth, and at the same time we look forward to the day 'when he shall come again in his glorious Majesty to judge both the quick and the dead.'

During Advent girls could tell the character of their young men either by the growth of onions stored in the chimney corner, or by pulling a stick from a faggot. In each case straightness signified honesty.